"Although I use Superman as a Christ-figure in my book *The Gospel from Outer Space*, Skelton, in his multitudinous parallels between the two, has left me at the starting gate. Seeing Christ as Superman can be an illuminating first step in seeing him as the God-man."

—**Robert Short,** bestselling author
of *The Gospel According to Peanuts*

* * ✳ * *

"Growing up, I had three moral guides: my family, Jesus, and Superman. The first Christopher Reeve movie was the Third Testament as far as I was concerned. This is the book I've been wanting to read since I was eight years old."

—**Mark Millar,** bestselling writer for *Superman Adventures, Ultimate X-Men, Marvel Knights Spider-Man,* and many other comic books

* * ✳ * *

"The need for us all to identify both the 'superhero' nature of Jesus—and the 'Jesus' nature of our superheroes—has never been greater. This book makes the relationship between the two undeniable.

"If you aren't afraid to think, I mean *really* think...pick up this book! It will open your mind to ideas and comparisons that are sure to both delight and challenge you. It's a sure bet to be sitting on the 'Kent' coffee table!"

—**John Schneider,** "Jonathan Kent"
on the TV series *Smallville;* cofounder
of the Children's Miracle Network

* * ✳ * *

"With superhero films taking in big box office, Skelton's approach couldn't be timelier."

—*CBA Marketplace* **magazine,** from
a review of *The Super Man Bible Study*

SUPER PARALLELS

Maybe you didn't know that...

* on the *Superman: The Movie* Special Edition DVD, the writer of the film says, "The metaphor was clearly there when Jor-El [the father] sends Superman to Earth, with God sending Christ to save humanity."

* on the *Smallville* pilot episode DVD, the director of the episode says, "I thought there were a lot of metaphors between Clark [Kent] and Jesus actually. And I tried to throw in as many of them as I could."

* in *Wizard* magazine, the director of *Superman Returns* says, "Superman is the Jesus Christ of superheroes"—and in *Entertainment Weekly,* he says that *Superman Returns* is "a story about what happens when messiahs come back..."

Keep turning the pages to discover what else you might have missed in the story of the World's Greatest Superhero!

* * * * *

THE GOSPEL ACCORDING TO
THE WORLD'S GREATEST
SUPERHERO

STEPHEN SKELTON

HARVEST HOUSE PUBLISHERS

EUGENE, OREGON

Cover by Terry Dugan Design, Minneapolis, Minnesota

Cover photo © Eamon O'Donoghue

THE GOSPEL ACCORDING TO THE WORLD'S GREATEST SUPERHERO
Copyright © 2006 by Stephen Skelton
Published by Harvest House Publishers
Eugene, Oregon 97402
www.harvesthousepublishers.com

Library of Congress Cataloging-in-Publication Data
Skelton, Stephen, 1972-
The gospel according to the world's greatest superhero / Steve Skelton.
    p. cm.
ISBN-13: 978-0-7369-1812-1 (pbk.)
ISBN-10: 0-7369-1812-4 (pbk.)
    1. Superman films—Moral and ethical aspects. 2. Motion pictures—Religious aspects—Christianity. I. Title.
PN1995.9.S77S54 2006
791.43'651—dc22   2005035220

Printed in the United States of America

06 07 08 09 10 11 12 13 14 / DP-CF / 10 9 8 7 6 5 4 3 2

To the Skelton family—whatever your last name may be.
I told you Earth would be better than Krypton!

and

To the participants in the making of
Superman: The Movie,
which made such an impact on a six-year-old boy
and pointed him toward the grander story
he longed to be a part of

Acknowledgments

My wife, Ashlee, and our two beautiful children, Rileigh and Harding (the younger of whom spoke thus when he was only two: *Me:* "Who is Superman?" *Harding:* "Clark Kent!" *Me:* "And who is Clark Kent?" *Harding:* "Daddy!").

My parents, Mickey and Joy, my older brother, David, and two younger sisters, AnneMarie and Emily, for their encouragement and, most often, indulgence.

Harvest House Director of Acquisitions Terry Glaspey for lending an ear not once, not twice, but three times before I pitched a project worth hearing; VP of Editorial Carolyn McCready for her infectious enthusiasm and quick support; VP of Marketing Barb Sherrill for being the other member of our *Smallville* fan convention; and Director of Marketing Katie Lane for putting the book in front of the right people in the right places.

Managing Editor Betty Fletcher for maintaining a steady hand despite the roller-coaster ride of a project that demanded more than its fair share of attention; Project Editor Paul Gossard for his seemingly limitless patience, kindness, and availability—all three of which I put to the test daily (in fact, he'll probably have to polish this very sentence).

Harvest House National Broadcast Publicist Christianne Debysingh and Radio Publicist Jeana Newman for letting the rest of the world hear about our book; Print/Internet Publicist Dave Bartlett for telling everyone about the top-secret chapter; Copywriter Nancy Shoptaw for revising my revisions of her copy—again and again.

Sales guys Rob Teigen—for entertaining endless out-of-the-box ways to sell the book (one of which might actually work, although I'm not sure which one)—and Jon Snell—for letting me attend important sales meetings like a tagalong little brother.

Writers David Bruce, Anton Karl Koslovic, and Michael Mautner—none of whom I've met—without whose knowledge and insight this book would be the poorer.

Graphic artist Eamon "The Extremist" O'Donoghue for our way-cool movie-poster-as-book-cover. Corbis representative Anthony Madrigal for his Herculean efforts in providing us with the images of Superman.

Endorsers Robert Short for his seminal *Gospel According to Peanuts*, which created the genre for this type of book over 40 years ago; John Schneider for his indelible portrayal of Jonathan Kent on *Smallville* (I'm *still* rooting for his resurrection); Mark Millar for being an authoritative voice on the intersection of comics, Christ, and Big Blue.

Lastly, the Unknown Person whose help I appreciate but whose name shall remain a mystery—you know who you are.

Contents

Superman Timeline
The Canon

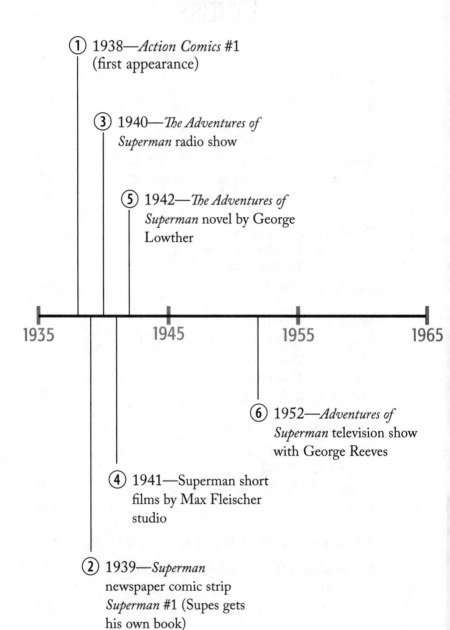

① 1938—*Action Comics* #1 (first appearance)

③ 1940—*The Adventures of Superman* radio show

⑤ 1942—*The Adventures of Superman* novel by George Lowther

1935   1945   1955   1965

⑥ 1952—*Adventures of Superman* television show with George Reeves

④ 1941—Superman short films by Max Fleischer studio

② 1939—*Superman* newspaper comic strip *Superman* #1 (Supes gets his own book)

Superman Timeline
The Canon

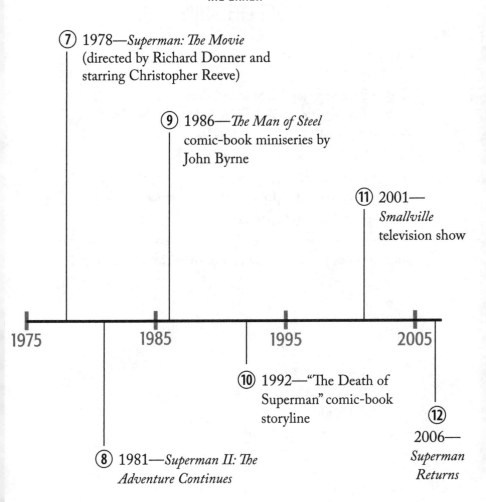

7 1978—*Superman: The Movie* (directed by Richard Donner and starring Christopher Reeve)

9 1986—*The Man of Steel* comic-book miniseries by John Byrne

11 2001— *Smallville* television show

1975   1985   1995   2005

10 1992—"The Death of Superman" comic-book storyline

12 2006— *Superman Returns*

8 1981—*Superman II: The Adventure Continues*

OTHER

1983
Superman III

1987
Superman IV: The Quest for Peace

1993
Lois & Clark: The New Adventures of Superman

List of Photos

Superman's Pal

I am Superman's pal. (Sorry, Jimmy Olsen.) I know because he's a friend.

But we didn't always know each other. By the time I came along, the *Superman* radio show was a thing of the past, as was the *Adventures of Superman* television show with George Reeves. Even the comic books were on the decline, with the heyday of the Silver Age—most of the '60s—behind them. It would take a miracle to bring Supes back to his former glory.

That miracle was the movie. I was six years old when we met. It was Christmastime 1978. For my generation worldwide, *Superman: The Movie* was like a religious experience. Even before we knew Superman was an actor named Christopher Reeve or there was a director behind the scenes named Richard Donner or a writer named Tom Mankiewicz—before we could learn all that, more immediately, more simply, more profoundly, we believed a man could fly.

It was epic, mythic, even evangelistic. A heavenly father sends his only son to save the Earth. The movie impacted us in ways we couldn't describe. It communicated a message that we

11

longed to hear and were desperate to have confirmed, but didn't yet comprehend why. We were children. Which is why the movie came to mean even more to us as we grew older. For me, it has meant the most in the last few years.

For the time being, we knew it brought people together, especially sons to fathers. Both of them saw in Superman their hero, their role model, what it could mean to be a man—to fight the good fight, to love others openly, to protect and provide. My dad, a super man, sat next to me in the dark and got lost in the vision as well. Both of us fully responding to everything. Neither of us fully understanding why.

After the movie, everyone applauded and we all stood up to go. Because the matinee was so packed, we still stood in our aisle. If not for that, we might have missed it.

Nowadays, not many recall that the "previews" were called "trailers" because they trailed the movie. This trailer was actually part of the original screenplay. The screen lit up again. Before my already overloaded eyes, new images of Superman appeared, images we had not seen in the movie. There were scenes of Clark and Lois in an embrace; the evil trio Zod, Non, and Ursa wreaking havoc; and most shockingly, Clark, having just been punched, with a bloody face! The adventure was continuing. I couldn't believe it. I couldn't wait.

Sequels

Three years later, *Superman II* didn't disappoint. To my youthful eyes, the 70-millimeter prints were huge, all-powerful, godlike. The dark theater, lit only by the bright, intense rainbow of colors from the screen, dominated by the actions of the people there, seemed like a place where anything could happen. And seeing our Man of Steel with that blood-streaked face raised my level of anxiety exponentially.

To a nine-year-old in 1981, the evil trio—Zod, Non, and Ursa—was just the safe side of scary, but still squirm-inducing. The battle in the city was unbelievable, inconceivable. The final fight in the fortress—finessed with a trick, the villains outsmarted rather than overpowered—deserved to be cheered. Seeing it today, I realize why I responded so; it is much more of a kids' movie than the first one. The second film is a true comic-book movie, whereas the first movie is more—it transcends its source.

Buoyed by the quality of the first two films, I stood in line for the third. Along with Reeve as Big Blue, comedian Richard Pryor appears as a computer whiz who gets plugged in with the wrong crowd. Even at the undiscriminating age of 11, I could tell something was off. The one bright spot was Annette O'Toole (as Lana Lang) who years later would shine in the role of Martha Kent on *Smallville*. Other than that, Pryor, for a funny man, wasn't that funny. Robert Vaughn, the human villain, fine in other things, was no Gene Hackman. And the supercomputer as supervillain failed to elicit much excitement. Although it was intriguing when the hero split in half—the dark side versus the light side—by and large, Superman had better things to be doing with his time. So did I.

Thus burned, I remember standing outside the movie theater in 1987, looking at the poster for *Superman IV: The Quest for Peace*—while waiting in line to buy tickets for another movie. Only recently did I watch the fourth film, almost two decades after its release. Boy, am I glad I waited—in fact, I should've gone longer. While it was great to see Reeve back in the suit, this silly movie simply doesn't merit much positive discussion. So bad was the fourth film that it accomplished what no other enemy had up until that point: It killed Superman. The big screen would wait nearly 20 years for him to return.

New Developments

In 1992, it happened for real. I remember seeing the evening news report on it. Superman was going to die. He was going to be beaten to death by a beast called Doomsday. Say goodbye to a friend while you still could.

The level of response from those wishing to pay their respects was off the charts. By the time the comic-book pages quit turning, a record-setting six million copies of the death issue had been sold. I have my copies of the collection. The storyline was extensive, stretching over nine months, before they finally brought him back.

I hoped they would make a movie out of it. And because of the tremendous amount of interest generated by Superman's death, Warner Bros. set to work on his resurrection for the theater, anticipating none of the usual problems with writing scripts, signing directors, and casting actors.

That was more than ten years ago. Superman would return to the small screen first. (And I don't mean *Lois & Clark*.)

Smallville was launched in 2001, and the strength of the pilot episode hooked me. I should have guessed what I later learned about the producers—they are huge fans of the original movie. Lead actor Tom Welling, our Young Man of Steel, has made such a strong showing that he has rightfully inherited the Superman television mantle from George Reeves. As the villain who proves the hero, Michael Rosenbaum as Lex Luthor has added new and compelling shades to a character established long ago. Some storylines have reinterpreted and augmented the mythology in ways that have even impacted the "canon," the sacred elements of the Superman saga.*

Cheering for the Good Guy

The recent success of *Smallville* seems to indicate that many, many people still buy into the fundamental principle of good the Superman story unabashedly celebrates. Yet it may not be enough. Over the years, we have become more selfish and cynical, a world of Luthor-worshippers. When things got dark, we got darker (something Superman would never do). In the darkness, we keep losing the vision of our bright future. And without that, we will perish spiritually.

A few of us are holdouts. We still are saddened when we hear of those less fortunate. Our sympathy goes out to them. We still

---

* For a listing of the items in the canon, see the timeline on pages 8–9.

cheer when the good guys win the good fight. For a moment, in our hearts, there is hope. And we know that the unbridled idealism, the assured triumph, the willingness to save that are embodied in Superman should be embodied in us.

Perhaps *Superman Returns* will remind us of that. The 20-year absence of the Man of Steel from the silver screen has created an incredible amount of anticipation. (If the positive word about the Bryan Singer production continues, I plan to be in line on opening weekend to see if the second coming is truly upon us.)

·   *   ✳   *   ·

Maybe you think salvation is too much to ask of a movie. I agree—the movie is only part of it. While the film must be good, it is only a vehicle for us to revisit a greater story. This is the story that, as children, we longed to hear and were desperate to have confirmed. Now we know why. It has the power to change lives. It has the power to heal, redeem, and reconcile. It is the Gospel—according to the World's Greatest Superhero.

I am Superman's pal. And I know something Jimmy Olsen doesn't, something you might not know either. His secret identity. His supersecret identity. I know who Superman really is. And it's better than Clark Kent, the secret identity he tells everybody about. Much better.

PART ONE

REVELATIONS

* * ✳ * *

Jesus spoke all these things to the crowd in parables; he did not say anything to them without using a parable.
MATTHEW 13:34

The problem of seeing not enough *in art-parable is far greater than the problem of seeing too much.*
ROBERT SHORT

It's been said that a parable is an earthly story with a heavenly meaning. The Superman saga is a heaven-to-earthly story with a heavenly meaning.

1

The Greatest Story Ever Re-Told

* * ✳ * *

Like many pals of the Man of Steel, for years I had heard rumors of superficial parallels between Superman and the Super Man, Jesus Christ. Although I'm inclined to find spiritual truth in worldly stories, for a long time I considered this an intriguing idea but one which was merely the opinion of those who chose to read that meaning into the story.

Then, a few years ago, I read a review of *Superman: The Movie* online at hollywoodjesus.com. The article, written by David Bruce, the creator of the Web site, began with the idea that people respond to Superman because he is a Christ figure—but then went on to outline incredible examples of how the gospel story was used as a template for the Superman story. By the time I had finished reading the review, this intriguing idea had graduated to an interesting argument.

Bruce's review spurred me to research that brought startling revelations. For instance, did you know that...

* Superman and his father share the last name of *El*—the

Hebrew word for *God*. Thus in the Superman story, when "El" the father sends "El" the son down to Earth, "God" the father sends "God" the son down to Earth.

* Superman's earthly parents, Martha and Jonathan, were modeled after the biblical parents Mary and Joseph—and as I later discovered, *Mary* and *Joseph* were the original names of the earthly parents.

* Superman's enemy is a villain called Lex Luthor, a name suspiciously like *Lucifer*. And both figures are fueled by the same all-consuming, all-corrupting hunger for power and glory.

I found these to be just the tip of a Kryptonian iceberg.

The Parallels Unfold

If the comic-book version of man's ancient question about the existence of a Higher Power asks, "Is it a bird? Is it a plane?" then the answer seemed clearer: "No, it's Jesus!" However, within my early research, I was also challenged by counterarguments. The foremost objection is that the parallels of Superman to Christ are coincidental at best and forced at worst because the creators of Superman were Jewish.

Jerry Siegel, the writer, and Joe Shuster, the illustrator—two Jewish teenagers—undeniably deserve their "created by" credit (although what they have to say about their inspiration for Superman is striking in itself). Yet I also found that the Superman story as it's popularly known is derived from a collection of works that is usually referred to as the Superman *canon* (a word loaded with religious symbolism)—and it was not told by only one person or even two.

For example, while Superman's full origin story came together over several years from multiple sources, the first time Siegel and Shuster told the tale in a newspaper comic strip, it was only a handful of panels before their version had progressed from Krypton to Earth and the super-child had grown to a Superman, ready for his first super adventure. Further on, the scripters of the *Adventures of Superman* television show were first to reveal that Superman's costume was created by Ma Kent from the blue, yellow, and red blankets in his spaceship.

In the early '40s, the Fleischer Studio produced a series of animated short films that added an essential scene, showing for the first time Clark Kent changing into Superman in a phone booth. The *Superman* radio show takes credit for the legendary motto "Faster than a speeding bullet! More powerful than a locomotive! Able to leap tall buildings in a single bound! Look, up in the sky! It's a bird! It's a plane! It's Superman!" Again, the radio scribes created the key characters of *Daily Planet* editor Perry White and cub reporter Jimmy Olsen. Momentously, it was the writers of the radio show who gave Superman his ability to fly—until that time, in the newspapers and comic books, he had merely jumped from place to place. And more pertinent to our purposes, I discovered that some of the storytellers in the Superman canon have deliberately worked to infuse the narrative with their religious, even Christic, intentions, as we will see.

As we follow the Superman story, we will see how it unfolds in many ways like the gospel story. That sequence also forms the progression of this book, which will deliver on its promise of revealing the many parallels between the two stories. In regard to the intentions of the creators, we will talk about the

The "Canon"

In this book, I have mostly focused on the main events of Superman's life, as drawn from a short roster of prominent sources that form the canonical story:

- early Jerry Siegel and Joe Shuster stories (from 1938 on)
- *The Adventures of Superman* radio show (1940)
- the Superman animated short films by Max Fleischer (1941)
- *The Adventures of Superman* novel by George Lowther (1942)
- *The Adventures of Superman* television show with George Reeves (1952)
- *Superman: The Movie,* directed by Richard Donner and starring Christopher Reeve (1978)
- *Superman II* (1981)
- *The Man of Steel* comic-book miniseries by John Byrne (1986)
- the "Death of Superman" comic-book storyline (1992 to 1993)
- more recent influences from the *Smallville* television show (2001) and the *Superman Returns* movie (2006)

See also the timeline on pages 8–9.

Superman storytellers who deliberately worked from the Christ story. Those intentions aside, we will see how the Superman story on its own exhibits instances of gospel borrowing too numerous to discount.

Then, for Christians who doubt we should use entertainment to further the gospel, we will take a look at the biblical precedents for using religious, secular—even pagan—entertainments to reveal spiritual truth. Further, for the unconvinced, who perceive the same parallels between the Superman story and the stories of religions besides Christianity, we will find these parallels lack significance. There are distinctions that make a difference—how Christ differs from Buddha or Krishna reveals how Superman differs from these figures too.

*   *   ✱   *   *

Superman is not Jesus Christ. But he is a Christ figure, a figure resembling Christ—as we all should be. That said, the story of Superman bears some incredible parallels to the story of the Super Man, Jesus Christ. Similarly, our own story should also grow to resemble that of Christ as we live to follow him.

Perhaps you have mostly thought of Christ as the suffering lamb. Why not the universal Hero? Jesus is both—as we will use Superman to illustrate. Perhaps you've been looking for a path to follow in your spiritual life. Here you may realize whose story you have actually been responding to and may accept him more fully into your life. Or perhaps you've been looking for a better means to talk with people who are attracted to Superman but who don't know their true Savior is the Super Man, Jesus Christ. All those possibilities you will find in this book.

If the movie *Superman Returns* tells us anything, it tells us that the Superman story is still being told, as is the story of the Christ who will return. Think of this book, then, as a concise collection of the facts that show the essential parallels between Superman and the Son of Man. Because the gospel story is the crucial story by which all humankind longs to define their lives, to the extent that the Superman story corresponds to the gospel story, the superhero from Krypton offers some soul's illumination, some heart's preparation. This is what I wish to communicate to you in *The Gospel According to the World's Greatest Superhero*, which is, I hope, at once a dim shadow and a bright reflection of the gospel of Jesus Christ.

2

A Reflection to Be Recognized

* * ✳ * *

For me, at first, the comparison of Superman to Jesus Christ raised three hesitations, which I found were shared by other people as well. They are…

* Does God use entertainment like this in the Bible?

* Shouldn't the gospel story stay in the Gospel?

* Isn't Christ above comparisons?

We'll touch on each to sharpen our perception for our super application.

God's Message in Art?

So where in the Bible can we find precedents for God using art, or even entertainment like Superman, to further his message? To gain an answer, we should understand God's love for creativity. To illustrate, consider that he introduces himself in the book of Genesis, through his actions, as the Creator. He does not introduce himself as the Lord, as Shepherd, as Father, or

God's Love for Artistry

In the "shadow" of God's own creativity, David the Poet King writes psalms. These are his songs, his art for pleasure, used to further the work of God. And of the later Hebrew prophets, writer Colin Harbinson suggests that their public displays are much like street theater, albeit with a divine patron of the artist.

as Savior[1]—four other prominent roles, any one of which he could have chosen to be known by first. And, based on just this much description—of him as the Creator—he then tells us we are created in his image.[2] Hence, we are all created to be creative, whether we would call ourselves artists or not.

Consider Bezalel, the first person we read of in Scripture to be invested with the Spirit of God.[3] What did Bezalel do to deserve such an honor—and what will he do with this unprecedented blessing? Is he going to prophesy? Is he going to perform a healing? Or even raise someone from the dead? All of these tasks sound worthy of the Spirit of God.

However, God has a different purpose. He invests Bezalel with his Spirit so Bezalel can create art. As God speaks with Moses on Mount Sinai, the Lord chooses Bezalel to create artistic designs for his tabernacle. Indeed, Bezalel means "in the shadow of God," which paints a beautiful picture of what happens when we act creatively: We stand in the presence of our Lord.

In the New Testament, with an inspired turn to pagan art, Paul quotes from the pagan poet Epimenides' *Cretica*, written in defense of the divinity of Zeus: "In him we live and move and have our being."[4] In the same sermon on the "Unknown God," Paul also quotes one line, "We are his offspring," shared by two more pagan poets, Aratus in his *Phaenomena* and Cleanthes in his *Hymn to Zeus*, the title of which speaks for both works—and says it all.

Later, in a letter to church members, Paul quotes from the pagan poet Menander in his *Thais*, a comedic theater play named after the most beautiful whore of the ancient world: "Bad company corrupts good character."[5] And still later, the apostle revisits *Cretica* for good measure: "Cretans are always liars, evil brutes, lazy gluttons"[6]—because they challenge the divinity of Zeus. Today, we would probably shun these three works of art for being blasphemous. So it is a good thing we were not there to dissuade Paul from creatively discerning the spiritual truth in these pagan entertainments. They offer a powerful testament on God's scriptural instruction for how we are to engage our world—and even the stories in it—with creativity. (You can thank Paul if Superman suddenly seems like the least of your entertainment worries!)

The Gospel in Everyday Stories?

Next, would God approve of having the gospel story retold through a comic-book story? This question springs from two assumptions: first, that common, popular story is not worthy of God, and next, that the gospel should only appear in the Gospels.

First, we should consider the way in which God uses story in the Bible—which is abundantly. When even a casual comparison is made between the Bible, the inspired Word of God, and fundamental texts of man-made religions, a significant difference in the delivery of the message (not to mention the message itself) quickly becomes apparent. In his "bibles," man largely provides a laundry list of behavioral directions—do this, don't do that. However, in the Holy Bible, God uses story to reveal truth—the Creation story, the Adam and Eve story, the Cain and Abel story, and so on. Surely this is the purpose for which the Creator created story: to be his chosen vehicle to reveal himself.

But even if this is true, wouldn't God frown on the reinterpretation of the gospel story outside of the Gospels—in the Superman story? If he did, he would also have to frown on

* David for his appropriation of Passion imagery to describe his own suffering in the book of Psalms

* Jonah in the belly of the whale for his symbolic (if not literal) death, burial, and resurrection

    *   Jesus himself for drawing parallels between himself and
       David and Jonah[7]

Clearly, God has a heart not only for story but for the creative
reflection of his story.

Christ in a Fictional Character?

Lastly, is it appropriate to see the figure of our Lord and Savior
Jesus Christ in the figure of a fictional superhero like Superman?
On this point, a crucial distinction must be made: Christ is Christ,
and a Christ *figure* is just that—not Christ but a reflection of
him. A Christ figure is not Christ any more than the image in
your mirror is the total you. Furthermore, to acknowledge the
similarities in your reflection in the mirror to you yourself does
not cheapen, or taint, or disprove the real you. And so it is with
Superman, the reflection, to Christ, the real person.

Remember, it was Christ who made Christ figures out of the
figurative prisoners we are to visit in jail.[8] If we refuse to consider
seeing Christ in any given thing or person, we risk missing how
Christ is using a particular thing to reach people. We may be
modern disciples, but we are also the disciples of Jesus' day, asking
the Lord why he speaks in parables.[9] Worse, when we do not
understand, we reject the stories. In limiting our perception, we
cut ourselves off from story as a vital testimonial tool in our work
of reconciliation, the ultimate way of serving that God has given
to each one of us.[10] Robert Short puts it this way for us today:

> We just as well could ask him [Jesus], "When did
> we see you in a film and did not listen to you or in
> a novel and did not learn from you? When did we
> see you in a painting and did not grieve with you
> or in a cartoon and did not laugh with you?"

Christ Figures Apart from Christ

Now, we should note that a fictional character can be a Christ figure and at the same time his own person—in fact, he must be. If a Christ figure cannot also be his own person—with his own thoughts, feelings, and actions apart from Christ—then he would not be a Christ figure, he would be Christ.

To better illustrate this point, consider the biblical precedent we have in the story of the loaned money.[11] A master going on a journey entrusts his money to his servants. As Jesus tells it, the master is a God figure, the loaned money represents God-given gifts, and the servants are us. The first servant receives five talents, the second servant receives two talents, and the third servant receives one talent. When the master returns, while he is pleased to find that the first two servants have doubled the money entrusted to them, it is not so with the third.

> Then the man who had received the one talent came. "Master," he said, "I knew that you are a hard man, harvesting where you have not sown and gathering where you have not scattered seed. So I was afraid and went out and hid your talent in the ground. See, here is what belongs to you." His master replied, "You wicked, lazy servant! So you knew that I harvest where I have not sown and gather where I have not scattered seed? Well then, you should have put my money on deposit with the bankers, so that when I returned I would have received it back with interest."[12]

The Ungodly God Figure

Look at the manner in which the master, the God figure, is portrayed. The third servant describes his master as a thief, harvesting where he has not sown and gathering where he has not scattered seed. More surprisingly, the master himself repeats the slanderous accusations without a denial. Although some might say that the master repeats the charges with a dubious note in his voice, there is nothing like a plain, outright refutation of the accusations—which you would think would be important to

Christ if he was concerned with a literal interpretation of his God figure.

By his example, we can see that the requirement of strict symmetry would bankrupt the appeal of a character as a God figure or Christ figure to anyone but believers. While a character that is both a master and a God *figure* can speak to both nonbeliever and believer, a character that is strictly *God* will appeal to only his followers. In addition, if we disqualify a character from having Christlike aspects solely because he does not act exactly like Christ, then we cut ourselves off from many opportunities to point out Christ in fictional characters that attract the attention of people who need him. Therefore—following the lead of Jesus—within the Superman story we must allow Clark Kent to be free to be a Christ figure *and,* at the same time, a "Clark figure."

Training Ourselves from Jesus' Own Stories

Having covered our three concerns, we have sharpened our perception to discern either the image or message of Christ in all things. We already have the permission to see the Creator in all creation. As Paul states of Jesus, "By him *all things* were created: things in heaven and on earth, visible and invisible, whether thrones or powers or rulers or authorities; *all things* were created by him and for him. He is before *all things,* and in him *all things* hold together."[13]

If we do not develop the perception to see Jesus in all things, then Christ may say of us also what he said of people who did not comprehend his parables:

> In them is fulfilled the prophecy of Isaiah: "You will be ever hearing but never understanding; you will be ever seeing but never perceiving. For this people's heart has become calloused; they hardly hear with their ears, and they have closed their eyes. Otherwise they might see with their eyes, and hear with their ears, understand with their hearts and turn, and I would heal them."[14]

By contrast, if we can see Jesus in all things, whether religious or secular (and Paul would add pagan), Christ will say of us, "Blessed are your eyes because they see, and your ears because they hear. For I tell you the truth, many prophets and righteous men longed to see what you see but did not see it, and to hear what you hear but did not hear it."[15]

Applying Parables

The perception to bring revelation through biblical imagery is what Christians need to use to capture the hearts and minds of seekers today. So how can we reveal spiritual truth through secular stories such as Superman? And why should we expect that people will respond? The parables of Christ offer an excellent tutorial on the use of secular stories to reveal spiritual truth.

To start, we should note that the parable characters never proclaim the good news, rarely mention God, and also engage in sinful behavior. This realization should remove any perceived curse on many secular stories and free them for us to use as modern parables. While there are still secular stories that deliver the wrong message, that spread damnable darkness instead of spiritual light, they are not so numerous as those that are simply secular and can be a vehicle for our use.

In fact, to say that a story like Superman can be completely secular or completely nonreligious is to say falsely humans can be on their own, that they can be in the service of themselves. The Christian knows people cannot serve two masters—"that which is God and that which is not God," as Short writes. Yet Christians have been duped into thinking that stories can be secular or nonreligious. In truth, we are not given that option. All people—including storytellers—must serve somebody other than themselves, because they work toward an end designed by a divine Other. It's either eternal salvation or eternal damnation. Though we continue using the word *secular* to mean "not overtly religious," we must also acknowledge that *all* stories are by nature religious—either positively or negatively so.

Why else would Jesus use such stories as he did, when surely literal-minded church members would not? Along with the above understanding, he made two obvious, key distinctions we often don't:

1.   A story character is not a real person.

2.   An example is not an endorsement.

First, while a story may reflect real life, it is in fact not real life. If a story character commits sinful actions, there is in fact no sin committed. Next, simply because a story is about, say, greed does not mean greed is approved. On these points, if we dramatized the parable of the prodigal son like a soap opera for modern church members—without telling them what we were dramatizing—we would likely not get past the son demanding his money so that he could spend it on wine, women, and song (and then waste the rest). If we were to act out what the lost son said and did in a realistic manner, no doubt many would take offense, turn their backs—and miss the redemptive message. To which we can only say, thank goodness the Lord did not tell this parable to them.

The Master Storyteller

This, however, is the genius of Jesus, the Master Storyteller. He tells a secular story without religious language—yet abundant in symbolic imagery. The people, especially those who are looking for truth, let their defenses down, identify with the story characters, and become more open to the spiritual truth the parable contains. Thus, Jesus brings revelation to their lives, sometimes even explaining the meaning of what they are responding to. In a similar pattern then, Christians today can use the symbolic language of modern stories to speak to people who might not listen otherwise. By pointing to the spiritual truth in a given story, we can help others understand *what* they are responding to, so they understand *why* they are responding to it.

*   *   ✳   *   *

So why do we respond to what we respond to? Because God made man in his own image. Thus, we have an essential longing to be with him, to be comforted by what is familiar to our deepest heart; and because Jesus Christ is "the image of the invisible God,"[16] it is his figure—and by extension, his story—we will respond to most strongly. To ensure our response, when God created us in his image, he also created us with his image in us. But it is a God-shaped blank, as Pascal puts it, a vacant hole in our hearts, until he fills it with himself. He has even made room for himself in that hole, eternal room: "He has also set eternity in the hearts of men; yet they cannot fathom what God has done from beginning to end."[17] So from birth we have eternity in our empty hearts—an *empty* eternity. No wonder we feel restless.

Here's the point. In our desperate search for something to fill Forever, nothing in the temporary world will do. In fact, it will take the one thing that is the exact size and shape of eternity: God, who we come to through Christ. However, until we are enlightened about our relationship to Christ, we will continue to scramble after, grasp at, anything that appears to have his power to heal us. This looks like a job for Superman.

The Human Dilemma

Robert Short uses the picture of a locked heart with a Christ-shaped keyhole. "Because the locks of our hearts are so desperate to get themselves unlocked and freed [so our hearts can be filled], improper keys (or idols or religions or false gods) will often be jammed into these locks with a force that can cause these keys to take on some of the actual contours of the only correct key–God and/or Christ himself. Our unconscious need for Christ is so strong that even our false gods will sometimes begin to resemble Christ."

3

...And God Created Superman

*   *   ✳   *   ·

In the 1930s, in the depths of the Depression Era, two Jewish teenagers, Jerry Siegel and Joe Shuster, were seeking a savior. Within their search for a fictional hero, we can recognize our search for a real one. As we've seen, while we instinctively look to the life of Christ to pattern our own lives after, from time to time we mistake false figures for the true image. This would explain why Siegel and Shuster, as they worked toward finding the figure that filled the void, created not one but three "Supermen."

"Pre-Supermen"

Their first "Superman" was a supervillain. In "The Reign of the Superman," a self-published story, a homeless man encounters a chemical from a meteor that gives him superpowers—mental, not physical. He uses this mind-control for evil, even disrupting a peace conference, until he brings the world to the brink of war. After a newspaper reporter prays to "the Creator of the threatened world...to blot out this blaspheming devil," the chemical wears off, the vagrant loses his powers, and he shuffles back into obscurity. And so the first "Superman" failed to make a lasting impression.

Superman scholar Michael Mautner notes the above wording of divine intervention "had the ring of the worship of Reform Judaism," a movement which advocates that Jews fully assimilate into their local culture, whose center in America has always been in Cleveland, Ohio—Siegel and Shuster's hometown. Mautner cites this early writing as support for the religious interpretation of much of the latter Superman imagery.

The second "Superman" was a good guy—but with no super-powers. In "The Superman," the crime fighter is big and strong but wholly human. In the estimation of Les Daniels, writer of *Superman: The Complete History*, "He was a generic character based on a variety of sources from the pulps and the strips." More significantly, though, Siegel had arrived at the realization that Superman should be good. Making Superman "virtuous rather than villainous was simply 'sensible.'"

The Superhero We Know

Finally, Siegel and Shuster's third "Superman" was the one destined to impact the world. In him, the superpowers and super-purpose come together. He is not the same as others because he overcame human weaknesses—both physically and spiritually. Yet he is not entirely different because he seeks to help humanity from a sense of being one of them. As Daniels puts it, "In presenting an otherworldly being, Siegel seems to have touched upon a mythical theme of universal significance." Superman had begun his journey toward Jesus.

That journey began this way. On a cold Ohio night, a sleepless Siegel, who had lost his father years earlier when a robber shot him at his store, was seized by a vision of a superhuman hero, a strongman that was more than a strong man, a god on earth. And it was early the next morning, when he rushed to his best friend Shuster, who, in his family's small, seldom-heated apartment, with hands gloved against the chill, sketched on cheap wrapping paper the first images of a new icon, a figure that would first inspire them and later the country and thereafter the world.

In the world during those years, Jews were being oppressed by Adolph Hitler in Europe. Superman, "Champion of the Oppressed," as one of the first newspaper strips proclaimed, seemed an answer to trouble both abroad and at home in an America betrayed by the fallible god of Commerce and beaten down by the Great Depression. Perhaps it is of little surprise that Superman would arise from such desperate surroundings. This is how people usually come to Christ—when their false gods have failed them and their hearts are broken open (so that he may enter in), and there is no other direction to look but up.

What Were They Thinking?

Of these Christic parallels, many may wonder, what would Superman's two teenage creators think? Indeed, what were they thinking—or about whom—when they created a savior with such universal, even eternal, appeal? In forming their Superman initially, the two inventors acknowledged that they consciously drew from their Jewish heritage. In fact, Siegel openly cited an Old Testament figure as an inspiration for Superman's astounding physical strength. In his words, Superman was made from the mold of "Samson, Hercules...all the strong men I had ever heard of rolled up into one, only more so."

Les Daniels maintains that Siegel and Shuster had made

Samson and Hercules

Two of the main influences for Superman prefigure the person of Christ.

From the book of Judges, Samson, whose name means "one who serves God," embodied several Christlike characteristics: His birth was foretold by an angel, he was a protector of Israel, his strength was divinely derived, and he sacrificed his life for his people—or as George Landow writes, "Samson, who gave his life for God's people, partially anticipates Christ, who repeats the action, endowing it with a deeper, more complete significance."

From Greek mythology, Hercules (also known as Herakles) also exhibited several Christic traits: He had a heavenly father (Zeus) and an earthly mother (Alcmene), he performed miraculous feats in the service of others, he was counseled by a spirit of divine wisdom (Athena), and he descended into and returned from a hell. Thus, these two figures, one biblical and one mythological, are significant as two prominent pre-Christ figures.

"a secular American messiah." However, Daniels then seems to contradict himself:

> Nothing of the kind was consciously on his [Siegel's] mind, apparently: his explanation for dropping Superman down from the sky was that "it just happened that way." And Shuster echoed him: "We just thought it was a good idea."

So it's natural to ask, if the creators of Superman did not *intend* Christic parallels, then isn't it true that Superman must not intrinsically *have* Christic parallels?

Inspiration Behind the Intention

However, if we assume that a story can only mean what its authors intended it to mean, we are committing what in literary criticism is referred to as the *intentional fallacy*. To illustrate, consider this personal application: You hear a love song that reminds you of a loved one. However, the author of that love song didn't know your loved one, so he couldn't have intended for his song to remind you of your loved one. Thus, according to this false logic, you are wrong in thinking that the love song reminds you of your loved one.

In addition, Short points out,

> One reason why we should never finally try to judge the meaning of a work of art on the basis of the artist's intention is this: Who knows what those intentions were? Apparently, artists themselves have difficulty knowing this. Plato's Socrates can tell us: "I went to the poets....I took them some of the most elaborate passages in their own writings, and asked what was the meaning of them....Will you believe me?...There is hardly a person present who would not have talked better about their poetry than they did themselves. Then I knew that not

by wisdom do poets write poetry, but by a sort of genius and inspiration."

Finally, the intention of God ("inspiration") is more important than the intention of the author. In this book, although we point out when the creators of the Superman canon worked with Christic intentions, this is not really necessary (though that confirmation can make a convincing argument for disbelievers and others). Rather, to discern the valid meaning of a story, we must hold it up against the ultimate truth, *God's* truth, and examine the points of confirmation or contradiction. Here, we can find the real value in what a creator says of his own work. His words have weight if he understands where his inspiration comes from and the truth it contains.

The First of Many

The Siegel and Shuster comic-book stories "spoke a symbolic language of hope and fear which readers intuitively appreciated," Mautner points out. Indeed, these stories of hope and fear were so appreciated that the comic-book industry boomed mainly because of the success of that single figure, Superman, first seen in June 1938. Thereafter, under the influence of this dynamic leader, an entire universe evolved of fantastic heroes. Call them Superman figures. And if we can see them as Superman figures, then we can see them as Christ figures. And because Christ inspires Superman and Superman inspires all other superheroes, we can see how Christ inspires all comic-book superheroes.

In 1939, Batman was invented to capitalize on Superman's success. In some ways, he was defined as the ideological opposite of his predecessor. While Superman is led by the love of his parents to save others, Batman is driven by the murder of his parents to seek revenge. Originally it was thus: Superman was a savior, Batman an avenger; Superman was optimistic, Batman pessimistic; Superman was the light, Batman the dark. It was only after sidekick Robin joined him (done to make Batman more appealing to children), that Batman became a more benevolent father figure—and sales doubled.

Symbolically, "father figure" may be a too-appropriate title for Batman. For some see in him an embodiment of Old Testament Hebrew Law with its "eye for an eye, tooth for a tooth" requirements. Within Trinitarian imagery, with Batman as the Father, Superman is, of course, once again, the Son—and if we relate the Holy Spirit to Sophia, the Greek word for wisdom personified as womanly,[1] then we will come to Wonder Woman.

In 1941, Wonder Woman, the third of the "big three," landed as the female equivalent of Superman. Rather than from heaven, she comes from "Paradise"—"Island," that is. Instead of by her father, she is sent by her mother. Her name is a feminine version of his: Wonder for Super, Woman for Man. Her costume even incorporates the same color scheme—blue, red, and yellow. And of course, she uses her lie-detecting lasso to fight for truth.

Then, nearly 25 years after Superman arrived, Spider-Man swung onto the scene with an origin story that features a separation from his first family, rearing by adoptive parents, secret identity as a mild-mannered common man, day job at a newspaper, red-and-blue superhero costume, and a similar-sounding superhero name. Even Spider-Man's famous credo, "With great power comes great responsibility," seems to echo a line from Superman's first newspaper serial strip: "Clark decided he must turn his titanic strength into channels that would benefit mankind." Not surprisingly, Spider-Man has been a tremendous success. (Indeed, he has engendered his own imitator, Daredevil—another character with an inspirational father, a drive to save others and, notably, a penchant for Catholic Christian crucifixes.)

Most recently, Stan Lee, creator of the phenomenally popular X-Men—who also invented the Fantastic Four, the Hulk, Spider-Man, and Daredevil among others—explains the universal appeal of the X-Men lies in the fact that they are hated because "they are different even though they are good and trying to help the world." He concludes frankly, "There's almost a little bit of a Jesus

Christ feeling in that." If only all earthly creators were so aware of the influence of their heavenly Creator.

*   *   ✳   *   *

In the years since 1938, many writers have had a hand in shaping the Superman mythology. In it, as Anton Karl Kozlovic points out, there have arisen many parallels to the gospel story, "parallels that incorporated direct character transpositions, sacred symbolism, verbal identifiers, Christic signifiers, divine coloring, biblical phraseology and scriptural allusions." Whew—pretty heady stuff for a comic-book character.

C.S. Lewis again provides insight as to how this has happened:

> People often wonder "What is the next step? When is the thing beyond man going to appear?" Imaginative writers try sometimes to picture this next step—the "Superman" as they call him.... [The] Christian view is precisely that the Next Step has already appeared....The first instance appeared in Palestine two thousand years ago....He is not merely a new man, one specimen of the species, but the new man. He is the origin and centre and life of all the new men.

Because of this, and because of the God-image deep in their own hearts, the custodians of Superman, in attempting to portray

Jewish and American Mythologies

In the 1930s, had Siegel and Shuster been raised in a more traditional Jewish surrounding, "they would have attached themselves to the passionate biblical and rabbinic symbols which form the core of Jewish education," according to Michael Mautner.

On the influence of these symbols in Jewish story (and history), C.S. Lewis writes, "The Hebrews, like other people, had mythology: but as they were the chosen people so their mythology was the chosen mythology—the mythology chosen by God to be the vehicle of the earliest sacred truths, the first step in that process which ends in the New Testament [with Christ] where truth has become completely historical."

So although they were born into that Jewish ethnic—and spiritual—heritage, because Siegel and Shuster were not raised in that cultural environment, Mautner recounts that they "gathered together the precepts of Americanism as transmitted by the public schools and molded them into a symbolic figure, a secular savior embodying nationalist ideals...Superman was a watered-down Christ, a Jesus for the Jews." What other Savior could they write about?

the first superhero, would inevitably be most satisfied with a figure that most closely resembled the Savior Hero. And the same applied to the worldwide audience that embraced him.

The revelation that Superman is the most vibrant Christ figure in the world today goes a long way toward explaining why this character continues to resonate so strongly with people—almost 70 years after he was first introduced. One of *People* magazine's listings of today's most prominent pop-culture icons, featuring the likes of Tom Cruise and Oprah Winfrey, puts Superman in the Top Ten. And the image of Superman they feature is an illustration, not an actor, emphasizing that it is a spiritual essence that appeals to us rather than a physical presence.

Superman, the Media Messiah, has now been a star of print, radio, television, film, and stage. His image has graced everything from breakfast cereals to bedsheets—and of course, he even has his own action figure. While he has inspired a multitude of imitators, he will always remain the world's first and favorite superhero...or "second," some might say.

PART TWO:

ORIGIN

*   *   ✳   *   *

The times are desperate. The plan is dramatic. The salvation of a people depends on it.

From above, a father sends his only son to Earth. To them, the Earth represents the ideals of rebirth, redemption, and restoration. The son is sent as an example of their way.

On Earth, his arrival is announced by a star from the sky. He is first seen by common folks, people of the earth. He is raised by adoptive parents in humble surroundings.

His earthly mother is called Mary. His earthly father is named Joseph. As God-fearing people, they would raise him always to be truthful, just, and caring. Because he is not of this world, he dwells among men an outsider. Yet he has a special destiny.

This is the story of two saviors. One is Jesus. The other is Superman.

4

The One and Only Son

*   *   ✳   *   *

*God so loved the world that he
gave his one and only Son.*

John 3:16

In the beginning, the first dramatic scenes of the Superman origin story are overflowing with biblical imagery, both visual and linguistic. Both types are important because they indicate an original, inherent inspiration—whether consciously acknowledged or not.

The home planet Krypton, doomed for cataclysmic destruction by fire, recalls the home planet Earth, doomed for cataclysmic destruction by flood. In the first newspaper serial, Krypton is destroyed as earthquakes shatter the surface and the core explodes outward. In ancient times, the Earth is decimated by flood as God opened both "the springs of the great deep" and "the floodgates of the heavens."[1]

In fact, this line of symbolism can travel even further along the biblical narrative. The spaceship bearing the Last Son of Krypton resembles the Ark carrying Noah and his family—both being the only survivors of previous civilizations. Indeed, within that same newspaper serial, the spaceship is originally referred to as an "Ark of Space."

At least one more Old Testament parallel can be seen in the image of an infant set adrift in a small vessel who would one day become a leader among his people. According to Scott Beatty, writing in *Superman: The Ultimate Guide to the Man of Steel,*

> The clear allusions to the biblical story of Moses were not lost on Jerry Siegel and Joe Shuster. They decided that, like the good son of Pharaoh, Superman would emerge from these humble beginnings to lead his people, from the townsfolk of Smallville to the millions of Metropolis and beyond to a better world.

On this point, we will briefly revisit our pre-Christ figures, because Moses is the preeminent one, more so than Samson and Hercules combined (see sidebar on page 37). The story of Moses can be found in Exodus and Numbers. At Moses' birth, Pharaoh ordered the death of Israelite children. Separated from his original family, he was raised under adoptive parents. He was destined to be a savior of his people. He was audibly called by the Lord to his ministry. His enemy strove to enslave his people. He performed miracles in God's name. He was the bearer of the law. He saw the glory of the Lord. And of course, as George Landow points out, " 'Moses leading the Children of God from Egyptian slavery into the promised land' acts as a type for 'Christ leading all men from spiritual slavery, sin, and ignorance into the heavenly kingdom.' " Indeed, the imagery of Jesus as the new Moses is a central theme of the Gospel of Matthew.

Farewell to Krypton

This presents yet another reason that, as the mythology continued to evolve, the symbolism of the Superman story ultimately, inexorably pointed to that of the Christ story. In fact, one of the flagship indicators of the Christic parallels within Superman can be found just before the infant, still under his Kryptonian name Kal-El, leaves Krypton.

Over time, the farewell words that the father speaks to his infant son Kal-El would undergo many revisions, additions, and refinements. Earlier versions had focused on the well-being of the child or the survival of his people through him. However in 1978, *Superman: The Movie*—the definitive version of the Superman story for generations of fans—would feature a benediction, which made nearly explicit much of the biblical imagery that had been used over the past 40 years in the origin story of Superman.

To establish the initial setting as presented in the movie, Anton Kozlovic notes that the color scheme for the entire planet is white, "the iconic signature color of the Divine,…which is biblically used to symbolize 'holiness and righteousness.'" In addition, through a marvelous visual effect, the Kryptonians wear clothes that glow brightly, recalling the description of clothes worn by angels, "clothes that gleamed like lightning."[2] Tom Mankiewicz, the scribe responsible for the final script, divulges, "On Krypton, I was intending it to be almost semi-biblical." Appropriately for a Christic parable, the first words come from the father Jor-El (played by the late Marlon Brando)—who is so much a God figure, even his hair is white: "This is no fantasy. No careless product of wild imagination." As John K. Muir recounts,

> Immediately before sending away his child, Jor-El and his people (angels?) have fought a war against an insurrectionist named Zod (Lucifer?), who is finally cast into a nether region (not Hell, but the Phantom Zone!).[3] Before being vanquished, this villain threatens to return one day to combat Jor-El

Marlon Brando, Susannah York, and Leo Quigley in _Superman: The Movie._ The family trinity as the Holy Trinity. "I wrote this long speech for Brando when he puts Superman in the capsule, and there are obvious allusions to God sending Christ to Earth: 'I sent them my only son.' " (Tom Mankiewicz, writer of _Superman: The Movie_).

and his heirs—an Armageddon that is highlighted in *Superman II.*[4]

During an "alien nativity scene," Kozlovic continues, "Kal-El 'is wrapped in swaddling clothes in a space-age manger which, with its sunburst arrangement of crystals surrounding it, very much resembles the way Christ is often portrayed in pictures and statues.'" He is now ready for his "voyage of rebirth inside the heart of a crystalline rocket that looked like a Christmas nativity star. This interstellar vehicle was variously described as 'a blend of crib and Magi star,' 'an unearthly manger,' or a 'little star-of-Bethlehem spaceship.'"

Words of Promise

It is within such a Kryptonian setting that Jor-El the father delivers to Kal-El the son a farewell speech that for many followers stands as a milestone in the revelation of the story of Superman as a mirror to the story of Jesus Christ:

> You will travel far, my little Kal-El, but we will never leave you, even in the face of our deaths. The richness of our lives shall be yours. All that I have, all that I've earned, everything I feel, all this and more I bequeath you, my son. You will carry me inside you all the days of your life. You will make my strength your own, see my life through your eyes, as your life will be seen through mine. The son becomes the father and the father the son.

Short comments, "At this point the script sounds like it might have been ghost-written by the author of the Gospel of John." Actual author Mankiewicz provides confirmation: "The metaphor was clearly there when Jor-El sends Superman to Earth with God sending Christ to save humanity."

Indeed, the metaphor is clearer than Mankiewicz might have known. For Superman, as mentioned earlier, is departing a planet bearing the name Krypton. *Krypton*—or its derivative forms—is a word used in the Greek New Testament to describe the kingdom of heaven as "hidden." At one point, the kingdom is compared to yeast hidden ("krypton") in the dough. And a few verses later, the kingdom is like treasure hidden ("krypton") in a field.[5] This second reference resonates strongly with the Superman origin imagery. When the infant Kal-El lands in the Kansas cornfield, he is then literally a treasure hidden in a field—a physical representation of the figurative description of the kingdom of heaven. To underscore the significance of this parallel, recall the kingdom of heaven began when Jesus entered the world.*

Divine Mythmaking

Apart from the "where" of Krypton, the "who" of the father and the son offers an even more striking example of biblical phraseology. In 1942, George Lowther, narrator, writer, and later director of the highly successful *Superman* radio show—a show that had a good deal of influence on the Man of Steel's origin story—wrote the first Superman novel, *The Adventures of Superman*. This novel "took a conscious approach to myth-making," as Mautner comments.

Originally, the father was named Jor-L and the son was named Kal-L. However, Lowther would transform the family name from "L" to "El," which was adopted by the comics and became canon. As one reviewer astutely noted, this was "curiously Hebraic-sounding alien." Profoundly, "El" is the Hebrew word for "God." (This is evident in names such as "El-Shaddai," meaning "God Almighty," for the Father; and "Immanuel," meaning "With us (is) God" for the Son.[7]) Thus, from this time forward, when

---

* Various other uses of "krypton" in the New Testament also offer interesting interpretations. Some seem particularly relevant to the Superman origin story. In one verse, Jesus is compared to a lamp that should not be kept in a place where it will be hidden ("krypton"). Another verse tells us that whatever is hidden ("krypton") is meant to be revealed. In Matthew, Jesus praises the Father because he has kept things hidden ("krypton") from the wise and learned and revealed them to little children.[6] Within our context, this is an intriguing use because the Superman story—the Gospel according to Superman—was first "hidden" in a comic book, ignored by the wise and learned but revealed to little children.

El the father sends El the son, God the Father sends God the Son—in the truest linguistic sense.

Completing the imagery of the Trinity here, with God the Father and God the Son thus represented, mother Lara (Susannah York)—"the keeper of the archives of Krypton," as revealed in the film *Superman II*, or a "vessel for Kryptonian wisdom, knowledge and other sagely advice" according to Kozlovic—is the de facto stand-in for the Holy Spirit as "the spirit of truth" that can guide one "into all truth."[8] The sorrow felt by Lara must echo on some level the sorrow felt by the Trinity in sending Christ to die for the sins of mankind: "He won't *be* one of them," she protests; "He will be odd, different," she laments with the infant in her arms, "Isolated. Alone."

*   *   ✴   *   *

What's in a Name?

The use of "El" in the Superman lexicon gives fresh meaning to standard phrases. For example, "Son of El" is "Son of God." "El of Krypton" is "God of Secret" ("secret" being another definition of "krypton"). Indeed, Jor-El's house is called the "House of El," while the biblical word "Bethel"–"beth" meaning "house"–gives the same connotation, "House of God."[9] This biblical translation indicates why "Bethel" is such a popular church name.

When El became the definitive family name, as Sarah Kozloff remarks, it edged "Jor-El" closer to "Jehovah." More momentous, the change gave "Kal-El" an even greater phonetic similarity to "Immanuel." Indeed, the transition indicated an interesting new translation. *Kalal* is the Hebrew word which means "to complete." Within this word, "kal" is a derivation of "kol," the Hebrew word for "all." Therefore, "kal" means "all" and "El," as established, means "God." Thus, as the Kryptonian ("Secret") alias of Superman, "Kal-El" is translated "All-God."

Just as Jesus was all-God and all-Man, the Superman imagery defines him as the same. Although from another world, Superman is not an "alien" as that term is commonly used in science fiction. In fact, the very first newspaper strip clearly states that "Krypton…bears a civilization of Supermen—beings which represent the *human race* at its ultimate peak of perfect development!" (emphasis added). Curiously, this imagery resonates with the delivered saints in their perfect bodies in heaven: "Our citizenship is in heaven. And we eagerly await a Savior from there, the Lord Jesus Christ, who, by the power that enables him to bring everything under his control, will transform our lowly bodies so that they will be like his glorious body."[10]

Later, the humanity of Superman was again established in the first issue of his own comic book. In *Superman* #1, on a page given to a "scientific explanation of Superman's amazing strength," the piece concludes: "It is not too far fetched to predict that some day our very own planet may be peopled entirely by Supermen!" Indeed, this would explain his first famous nickname "The Man of Tomorrow." But even his name tells us he is human: the son is not destined to become known as "Super-alien," but rather "Super-man."

5

The Star Child

*   *   ✳   *   *

*God did not send his Son into the world
to condemn the world, but to save
the world through him.*

John 3:17

As we've seen, *Superman: The Movie* is a thinly veiled version of the story of Jesus Christ. Director Richard Donner downplayed Superman's allegorical divinity but was forced to acknowledge it. He relates,

> I had life threats, because people accused me of approaching [Marlon] Brando [the actor portraying Jor-El] as God and his son as Jesus....We had Scotland Yard, the FBI, and the LAPD looking into them. I literally had people saying that my blood would run in the streets for doing that.

Whether the objections were made to the *parallels* to Jesus or to the very *indication* of Jesus, it's unclear. Regardless of how he is talked about, some would prefer that Jesus not be talked about at all. Only later did writer Tom Mankiewicz feel comfortable admitting to the subtext, saying, "It's a motif I had done at the beginning when Brando sent Chris [Reeve, the actor portraying the adult Superman] to Earth and said, 'I send them my only son.' It was God sending Christ to Earth."

This motif continues in the movie as the space manger nears Kansas. Heading to the east, the shining starship suddenly changes course to the west, descending to an immaculate landing in that predestined cornfield. As Kozlovic comments, the star imagery here recalls the birth announcement of Christ by "his star in the east" which acted by divine intervention to show "where the child was.[1] The Star of Bethlehem as a signpost of baby Jesus' location is forever linked together in Christian folklore." (Conspicuously, in the comic books, "Kal-El" is Kryptonian for "Star Child.") The toddler emerges from the starship naked, symbolic of birth.

The Star Child's Parents

That Superman is human helps the farming couple who becomes his earthly parents to relate to him—an adoption process Scott Beatty described as "an interstellar orphan from a dying world blasted to Earth in a tiny rocket to be raised by simple God-fearing folk." But who are these "God-fearing folk"?

Originally, the father is named Jonathan, and the mother is, suitably, named Mary.* Later, without explanation, "Mary" would be renamed "Martha." Perhaps, this was an attempt to distance the mother of "Clark" (as the Kents christen the infant) from such a blatant allusion to the mother of Jesus. However, Jonathan Kent continues to possess a revelatory middle name: "Joseph." Thus,

---

* According to Mautner, Lowther also altered these names in his novel, as Jonathan was changed "to Eben, a form of Abraham, the mythical patriarch of Biblical Israel," while "Mary Kent became the matriarch Sarah." However, apart from a brief reappearance in the first episode of the *Adventures of Superman* television show, the names "Eben" and "Sarah" did not stick.

the earthly fathers of Jesus and Clark share a name. In fact, these latter-day "God-fearing folk" give the same middle name to Clark, "Joseph." (Jesus Christ and Clark Joseph. J.C. meet C.J.)

Kozlovic highlights the similarities between the parents of Christ and Clark: "Mary and Joseph were good and pious but of (a) lowly birth (i.e., non-powerful); (b) lowly station (i.e., vocationally, a carpenter and his wife); and (c) living in an unimportant location." Given their humble place in life, it is noticeable that in most presentations of the origin story, including *Superman: The Movie*, when the parents find the child, these farming folks are dressed in their "church-best" clothes, "thus implying Christian piousness on a Sunday," the most logical day of the week to find a Christ figure. As farmers, the Kents are both carpenters and shepherds, two resonant biblical professions: Joseph the earthly father of Jesus is a carpenter, and shepherds are the first to find the small Savior.

Resonances with the Bible

Kozlovic also notes how Martha Kent resonates with the biblical Martha: a follower of Christ who welcomes Jesus into her house and "was both careful and troubled."[2] Martha Kent's middle name was revealed to be Clark, "thus indicating that 'Clark Kent' was subsequently named after his surrogate mother not father," recalling the emphasis that Jesus was strictly the son of his earthly mother not father.

Based on her original appearance as an older lady—the traditional "Ma Kent" depiction—other biblical parallels have also been applied to Martha. Barren women who are given children by God is a prominent biblical motif, as evidenced by Sarah, Rebekah, Elizabeth, and Manoah's unnamed wife, the mother of Samson.[3] In *Superman: The Movie*, when Martha and her husband discover the boy, she confesses, "All these years, as happy as we've been, how I prayed and prayed the Good Lord would see fit to give us a child." She interprets this miraculous arrival from the heavens as the answer to her prayers.

As noted, Jonathan shares the name "Joseph" with the earthly father of Christ. Biblically, "Joseph" means "God increases," while "Jonathan" means "God has given." The similarities between the two figures continue when Joseph hesitates to claim the child at first[4] and Jonathan is also given pause in *Superman: The Movie*. And later, as a moral man who would be an earthly example to his adopted son, the life of Joseph provides the template for the life of Jonathan.

Biblical scholars speculate that Joseph dies when Jesus is still a young man—he is last mentioned when Jesus is 12 years old. Originally Jonathan also dies when Clark is still a teenager. However, in more recent years, along with a reduction in age for Martha Kent, Jonathan would be revised—in fact, revived—as their entire hometown of Smallville would experience something of a resurrection.

So How Did They Die—Or Did They?

Once upon a time, in the 1939 Siegel and Shuster telling in *Superman* #1, the Kents live and die in the little town of Smallville, before their special boy has become a Superman. After this, in George Lowther's 1942 novel *The Adventures of Superman,* the story was retold and the first Kent to go was Jonathan when he suffers a coronary and dies. In this version of the story, as the panicked Clark physically rushes Pa to the hospital, he discovers he can fly!

In 1963, the third time the Kents were rashly killed off, they weren't even in Smallville but on a Caribbean vacation. Both contract a fatal tropical disease and expire in *Superman* #161, "The Last Days of Ma and Pa Kent!" In 1978, *Superman: The Movie* seemed to settle the issue of Jonathan's demise for a few years when it depicted him succumbing to a heart attack. In this version, we are given to know that Pa (Glenn Ford) receives a Christian burial, as Ma (Phyllis Thaxter) stands at his graveside wearing a necklace with a cross and clutching a red-edged Bible.

However, in 1986, the origin story was revised for a relaunch of

Tom Welling, who plays the young Man of Steel in the *Smallville* television series. A typical example of the Christic-laced dialog: *Lex:* "Clark, you can't save the world. All you'll end up with is a Messiah complex and a lot of enemies." *Clark:* "I saved you, didn't I? That turned out all right." (From "Kinetic," episode #13.)

the Superman comic-book lines, and this time it was decided that Clark could benefit from the continued presence of the Kents as his spiritual "allies and anchors," according to Les Daniels. Good thing, too—it was beginning to look like Clark was the only Kent who could make it out of that small town alive.

A Humble Advent

Within the imagery of the Superman story as the Jesus story, Smallville is a stand-in for the small villages of Bethlehem and later Nazareth. Most recently, the contemporary source of Smallville mythology comes from the popular television show of the same name. When *Smallville* first appeared in 2001, it was the most-watched premiere in the history of its network, and as the show continued to run, it was among the highest-rated series to air on the network. For their story of the future Superman, the producers of *Smallville* set their version in present day with Martha and Jonathan as 40-somethings and Clark as a teenager in high school.

Smallville pilot director David Nutter professed his preference for instilling—or revealing—Christic imagery in the Superman story when he admitted, "There's a certain image that I think everyone has in their mind's eye of what Clark Kent should look like. For me, it's like, 'Who are you going to cast to be Jesus Christ...?'" Given that, another element of this new story is particularly intriguing. Superman's spaceship is ushered to Earth by a meteor shower, which not only infests the town with Kryptonian rock remnants but will later invest some townsfolk with superpowers. This *kryptonite*—radioactive pieces of Krypton—will provide Clark (Tom Welling) with a perpetual supply of worthy adversaries. More importantly, the producers use this plot device to make a moral commentary on the fallen state of man—in contrast to the repentance, redemption, and salvation offered by Clark. As executive producer Alfred Gough explains, "The power sort of enhances the sin. So they're not monsters in terms of makeup and stuff, but it comes from personal demons and things like that."

In an interesting twist to this version, the meteor shower that brings Clark to Earth also brings Judgment Day to Smallville as the burning boulder-size rocks wreck buildings, destroy cars, and take lives—among them, the parents of Lana Lang (Kristin Kreuk), the girlfriend Clark will pine for. This imagery heralds the modern-day Clark with the symbolism of the second coming of Christ, "when the Lord Jesus is revealed from heaven in blazing fire" to "punish those who do not know God...with everlasting destruction."[5] When the Kents first discover Clark, Jonathan (John Schneider) hesitates: "What are we supposed to tell people, 'We found him out in a field?'" To which, Martha (Annette O'Toole) replies, "We didn't find him. He found us," immediately casting the infant Clark in the role of Savior.

Images of a Savior

After this dramatic introduction, later in the pilot episode, Clark and Lana visit the graveside of Lana's parents. As if to reconfirm his Savior status, Clark stands by chance before an angel statue, framing himself with the wings to either side, the wings appearing for a moment to belong to Clark. Of this angelic imagery, pilot director Nutter confirms that, rather than having happened by accident, "That's in the script, him standing by the angel. I will not take credit for that."

Nevertheless, with the above fundamentals noted, the defining moment for the pilot episode—and perhaps the entire series—comes late in the first story. It is a scene so rife with iconography as to take one's breath: an overt religious image, startling in its familiarity, at once brazen yet fitting.

Within the story, the football bullies inadvertently weaken Clark with kryptonite, which is poisonous to him. The jocks then take Clark, as the victim of an annual school prank, to the middle of a cornfield and tie him to a scarecrow mast. To complete his humiliation, they strip him to his boxer shorts and paint a red "S" on his chest—for Smallville High.

Of course, when a body is mounted on a scarecrow mast, the image resembles a crucifixion. Thus, the teenage Christ figure is caught in a scene portending the sacrificial death that would bring salvation to the world. Notably, this image was included in the montage that covered the opening credits and appeared at the beginning of each episode for the first four seasons.

Suffering, Sacrificial Savior

Obviously, the reason the image of Clark as a suffering, sacrificial savior resonates with us is Christ. However, this same appeal applies whether in the Superman story or in other hero stories that feature Christ's image. As Louis Markos paraphrases C.S. Lewis,

> In the person of Christ we encounter a figure whose life, death, and resurrection, far from standing in opposition to the mythic heroes of paganism, in fact present a literal, historical fulfillment of what all those earlier myths were really about.

Lewis himself makes an important distinction between the Christian Incarnation—the act of the Son of God voluntarily assuming a human life—and the pagan myth of a god becoming man (as it has appeared in such origin stories in multiple cultures throughout history, and by extension, in the Superman origin story). He writes,

---

Crucifixion Imagery in the Superman Story

Does the use of the image of the crucifixion of Christ in the Superman saga come dangerously close to mockery? After all, one is fact, one is fiction. We may forget, though, that a story may be fictional but contain truth. Indeed, the real worth of a story can be measured by how it brings us closer to *the truth*—by which we mean the truth of God from "the God of truth."[6] God's truth is the only truth; whenever we hear truth, it is God's truth, whether we hear it through pastors or pagans.

This applies not only to stories that feature Christ figures prominently, but also to stories that contain subtle spiritual truth. The parables of Christ are an excellent example of the latter, as we saw in chapter 2. Just as the theme of all Scripture is Christ because he is the one to which all Scripture points, so the theme of all truth is God because he is the one from which all truth originates. What we call "spiritual truth" is simply *truth that knows where it comes from*, so it often speaks in the language of the church, in religious words and images.

As myth transcends thought, Incarnation transcends myth. The heart of Christianity is a myth which is also a fact. The old myth of the Dying God, without ceasing to be a myth, comes down from the heaven of legend and imagination to the earth of history.

Lewis further explains,

It happens—at a particular date, in a particular place, followed by definable historical consequences. We pass from Balder and Osiris, dying nobody knows when or where, to a historical Person crucified (it is all in order) under Pontius Pilate. By becoming fact it does not cease to be myth: that is the miracle.

In highlighting historical fact, Lewis begins to provide Christians with their apologetics (or defense) of the true Christ story—even as we view it through the fictional Superman story.

* * ✳ * ·

Perhaps the final confirmation on the importance of the crucifixion image to the *Smallville* story came when it was time to choose the cover art for the DVD box set of *Smallville—The Complete First Season*. There on the front cover, as the central image of the inaugural season, is Clark on the scarecrow mast, our teenage Christ figure on that makeshift cross—stripped and marked, humbled but not humiliated, resolute and noble, with eyes turned heavenward and head held up to the future, his and ours.

6

"You Are Here for a Reason"

* * ✳ * *

A voice from heaven said, "This is my Son,
whom I love; with him I am well pleased."

MATTHEW 3:17

As alluded to above, the story of Jesus' childhood proceeds briefly from being born in the manger to speaking in the temple at age 12 to being baptized into his ministry at age 30. Because not much is written about the formative years of Christ, apparently the producers of *Smallville* are giving it a shot.

An American Passion Drama

In *Smallville*, as exemplified earlier by the scarecrow/crucifixion scene, Christic imagery abounds.* And in its entirety, the plot of

---

* Consider the religious resonance of *Smallville* episode titles such as "Prodigal" (#36), "Calling" (#43), "Exodus" (#44), "Hereafter" (#56), "Resurrection" (#59), "Truth" (#62), "Covenant" (#67), "Devoted" (#70), "Sacred" (#81), "Spirit" (#84), "Forever" (#87), "Mortal" (#90), "Reckoning (#100), "Tomb" (#102), and "Mercy" (#107). In addition, the show's theme song is entitled "Somebody Save Me."

the *Smallville* pilot follows the Passion play—the drama on the suffering and crucifixion of Christ. Within the episode, the scarecrow/crucifixion scene is especially significant because this event is foreshadowed, built to and delivered as the culmination of one of the main story lines. As the story line begins, Clark and his best friend Pete (Sam Jones III) consider joining the football team, figuring this will preclude them from the feared yearly scarecrow prank. However, because Jonathan cautions that Clark could hurt others, Clark then refuses to join the team on the counsel of his father—like Jesus, limiting his power, acknowledging his destiny and facing the threat of his impending doom.

Further into the episode, Clark pleads with his father, "I'd give anything to be normal." Still later, he withdraws from his parents to a graveyard where he weeps. These actions recall when Christ withdraws to a grove to pray, "Father...take this cup from me." At that time, as the Scripture records, an angel appears to strengthen him.[1] Likewise, an angel (statue) stands behind Clark when he rises to his feet. There, Lana Lang discovers him as she comes to lay flowers on her parents' grave. Figuratively, Lana introduces Clark to her parents, then remarks that without them she has always felt alone. To comfort her, Clark listens to the silence of the cemetery and then says, "Your mom wants you to know that you're never alone. She's always looking over you, no matter what," reclaiming his role as the servant Savior.

Near the end, on the makeshift cross, Clark struggles under the burden of a necklace containing kryptonite. Remember that kryptonite is a stand-in for sin: As explained earlier by executive producer Gough, kryptonite empowers personal demons. Clark asks for help from the first person to appear: the villain of the story, a past victim of the scarecrow cross now seeking deadly revenge. The villain appears to the left of the cross, just as tradition places the first thief on the cross to the left of Christ. He mocks Clark, telling him he is safer where he is—echoing the mocking of the first thief at the crucifixion.[2]

The second person to find Clark is Lex Luthor (Michael

Rosenbaum), a friend at this point in the *Smallville* mythology. He appears to the right of Clark, just as tradition puts the good thief to the right of Christ. Lex asks, "Who did this to you?" Amazingly, Clark answers, "It doesn't matter"—mirroring Christ's plea to forgive his crucifiers.[3] In a miniature version of the death, burial, and resurrection,[4] as Clark drops from the cross (death) and lands face-down in the dirt (burial), the kryptonite necklace (sin) falls away powerless, and he regains his superhuman strength (resurrection).

In a similar pattern to the principals involved in making *Superman: The Movie*, *Smallville* executive producer Gough originally gave an alternate explanation for the scarecrow/crucifixion imagery. Of the stripped and marked Clark, Gough concludes simply, "Visually, it's Superman in his underwear with an 'S' on his chest." However, a little later director Nutter offers, "I thought there were a lot of metaphors between Clark and Jesus actually. And I tried to throw in as many of them as I could." Strong pitching arm.

The Reason He Came

As Clark grows older, in *Superman: The Movie*, Jonathan tells him, "You are here for a reason"—and the same could be said of Jesus and of us. Shortly thereafter, Clark hears the call of a green crystal from his ship; the crystal contains the spirit of his true father. (Green is the biblical color for growth.) In this, the crystal represents both the voice of God and the physical Holy Spirit—which are present at Jesus' baptism as God speaks and the dove descends.[5] Just as the voice and the dove confirm Christ, then send him into the desert,[6] so the green crystal confirms Clark, then sends him into the arctic. Thus, Clark, like Jesus, is sent on the journey to prepare for his purpose.

In the Gospel, the Spirit leads Jesus into the desert wilderness for solitude.[7] Likewise, in the corresponding arctic wilderness, the crystal creates an ice fortress for Clark's solitude, the "Fortress of Solitude." Here, Clark is tested over an extended period of time without sign of food while he is attended by the spirit of his father. In the Bible, we see a set of occurrences with nearly the same imagery—Jesus is tested in the wilderness, where he fasts and is attended by angels.[8] In regard to the Fortress of Solitude Kozlovic reasons that it "was a heavenly abode on Earth and thus a fit place for a spiritual entity to reside within." Inside the divinely white fortress, Clark communes with his father, reflects on his life, and focuses on the good fight. Through all of this, we see that the cathedral fortress most closely resembles a church—truly "his father's house," one equipped with pools of baptismal waters, from which will rise a new man.

In the shooting script of the film, Jor-El further confirms his association with God the Father, showing a conspicuous concern for moral instruction:

> There are questions to be asked and it is time you do so. Here in this fortress of solitude we shall try to find the answers together. How does a good man live? What is virtue? When does a man's obligation to those around him exceed his obligation to himself?

Again from the shooting script, Jor-El next extols the benefits of ethical conduct:

> The virtuous spirit has no need for thanks or approval. Only the certain conviction that what has been done is right. Develop such conviction in yourself, Kal-El. The human heart on your planet is still subject to small jealousies, lies, and monstrous deceptions. Resist these temptations as you inevitably find them—and your ethical power will then properly outweigh your physical advantage over others.

Humorously, one critic refers to Clark's training as "a twelve-year spiritual retreat." About this time, Christ lends to Clark one other major origin story event—early in his mission, Clark encounters his archenemy. Whereas Christ meets Lucifer, Clark meets Lex Luthor.

The Great Enemy

In the television series *Smallville,* as mentioned above, Lex Luthor is a friend of Clark Kent. In fact, in the pilot episode, Lex is the first life Clark saves. When Lex loses control of his car, he hits Clark walking across a bridge, plunging the two young men into the river below—a baptism, literally by water and spiritually by fire, for both. Afterward, Lex tries to reward Clark with a new truck, underlining his Lucifer-like focus on material possessions. However, Jonathan—in this instance, father figure and Father figure—counsels Clark he can't keep it. Later, Lex tells Clark that when his heart stopped after the crash, he found himself flying over Smallville and saw a new beginning for himself. Then Clark resuscitated Lex, brought him back to life, back down to earth—recalling a heaven-dwelling Lucifer cast down to the ground. (Nevertheless, remember that in the scarecrow/crucifixion scene, the person that saves Clark from this cross is Lex. As the hymn tells us, "He could have called ten thousand angels"—but for now, the image of one still-true archangel will do.)

According to Alfred Gough, *Smallville* is as much the story of how Lex becomes a supervillain as it is how Clark becomes a superhero. That is to say, Lex is portrayed as such a good guy, and his friendship with Clark holds such promise, we are riveted in dreadful expectation of the inevitable fall when Lex will turn to the dark side. As Gough reveals, Clark is caught between Jonathan and Lex, "these two titans, basically, who are going to, all through the course of the series, be fighting for Clark's soul." Literally, this Lex is an auspicious young man who will valiantly fight his inner demons, and though he may win a few battles will ultimately lose the war—along with his soul.

To illustrate this, Lex experiences an unfolding vision—seen twice in the series so far (episodes #6 and #76)—of a future that torments and terrifies him. In the first vision, he is president, dressed in a white suit. He walks out the door of the Oval Office and into a field of dandelions. He reaches out his hand and they turn black, disintegrating, revealing underneath a landscape of scorched skeletons. He grins. Thunder rolls down from above. He looks up into a red storm cloud. Droplets of blood rain down on his white suit. The vision ends. In the second vision, Lex is again standing in the Oval Office in a white suit. This time, we see nuclear missiles launched from U.S. soil. As before, Lex walks to the door and opens it. A bright light reflects on his face. From a view above America, we come to an understanding of Lex's demonic actions. The U.S. missiles fly up, turn, and hit U.S. soil. Lex has brought Armageddon to America. The vision ends again, for now.

Allegorically, this is our Enemy, that fallen rebel archangel Lucifer, as he existed in heaven before succumbing to his lust for power and glory and being cast down. For just as surely as Superman is a Christ figure, Lex Luthor is a Lucifer figure ("Lex Lucifer"). On occasion, to prove a point, Lex actually quotes Scripture to Clark—and the imagery recalls both the time Lucifer spent in heaven and, later, the time he quotes Scripture to Christ at the start of his ministry.[9] In a *Smallville* episode entitled "Aqua" (#92), Clark relates to Lex some scathing accusations made against his company. "He accused LuthorCorp of being evil. And you being just short of the Devil." To which Lex replies with a sarcastic smirk, "Well, you didn't tell him about my pitchfork, did you?"

A Light to Show the Way

In *Superman: The Movie,* Clark begins his mission as Superman at age 30—the same age that Jesus starts his public ministry as the Messiah.[10] At this time, Jor-El the father declares the earthly purpose of his son. Over the years, various purposes on Earth have been assigned to Kal-El, such as recreating his native civilization or, as a much darker directive, world dominance. However, in the shooting script of the movie, as seen below, the reasons become extremely, even divinely, altruistic. The son is sent to use his strength to serve, never forgetting his special birthright, to be a light to show the way to great goodness.

In addition, as Kozlovic cites, the speech is "quite explicit in its use of [the Gospel of John's] language about the relationship between the Father and Son," paraphrasing two of the apostle's well-known phrases: "I am the light of the world," and, "God so loved the world that he gave his one and only Son."[11] As Jor-El commands,

> It is now time for you to rejoin your new world and to serve its collective humanity. Live as one of them, Kal-El, to discover where your strength and your power are needed. But always hold in your heart the pride of your special heritage. Your being is both separate and your own, but I have caused your earthly presence and must share responsibility for your actions. They can be a great people, Kal-El—they wish to be. They only lack the light to show the way. For this reason above all, their capacity for good, I have sent them you—my only son.

With these words, Superman is launched on his mission—or is it, ministry?

Clark Kent's Messianic Identity

Despite the introduction of his public persona as Superman, our hero will continue to maintain the integrity of his earthly name, "Clark Kent." Aptly, "Clark" means "cleric"—a clergyman, or pastor. And as Gary Engle points out, "Kent is a form of the Hebrew *Kana* [or KNA]. In its k-n-t form, the word appears in the Bible, meaning 'I have found a son.'"

Even more striking, W.L. Glick notes that another derivation from the Hebrew word *Kana* is the Greek word *Krista*. Its English form, the word *Christ*, "is the best-known example of the inner meanings of the name. The Son of God, taking his Father's name, as His last name." Few names could have a richer or more apt meaning than Clark Kent—"Cleric Christ."

PART THREE

MISSION

* * ✳ * *

He is raised in a small town. He is destined to save the world. He is about to begin his work.

Though intended for greatness, he patiently waits to fulfill his purpose at age 30. To initiate his ministry, the spirit of his heavenly father takes on a physical form and sends him into the wilderness.

Early on, he encounters his archenemy. This is a villain who lusts for glory and power. One who tempts with earthly rewards—to no avail. Having passed the test, our hero answers his calling. In his public ministry, he will keep a secret identity.

He will see all men as equal. He will treat all men with love. He will use his strength, both physical and moral, to benefit others, to serve and to save, to lead the people of today toward the brightest tomorrow.

7

A Never-Ending Battle for Truth

*   *   ✳   *   *

*Jesus returned to Galilee in the power
of the Spirit...*

Luke 4:14

For Superman, his mission—in motivation, in action, in impact—bears similarities both symbolic and concrete to the ministry of Jesus Christ. In *Superman: The Movie,* Superman emerges from the Fortress of Solitude (church) with what Kozlovic calls "a clear idea of his messianic mission to battle evil and save Earth from its own foolishness."

Soon after reentering society, Superman begins performing miraculous deeds reminiscent of the miracles of Christ:

* Jesus heals the sick and even the dead;[1] Superman saves Lois Lane (Margot Kidder) from death—twice in his first week (from a mugger and from a helicopter,

the latter of which a newscaster calls "a miraculous saving").

* Christ rescues the disciples in a boat in a storm;[2] Superman rescues the President in a plane in a storm.

* Jesus walks on water;[3] Superman flies through the air.

At one point, in an action befitting a Savior who is "gentle and humble in heart,"[4] Superman rescues a kitten from a tree, a scene that was deliberately "designed to demonstrate Superman's humility and humanity," according to Kozlovic. Upon depositing a caught cat burglar with a police officer, Superman offers spiritual advice to benefit both: "They say confession is good for the soul? I'd listen to this man."

Who Is He?

In *Superman: The Movie*, a reporter summarizes the fundamental question—"True or false? Miracle or fraud? The answer is up to you. Man or myth." Christ asks more succinctly, "Who do you say I am?"[5]

The Source of Truth

Even the language used in their respective mission statements resonates the latter with the former: Superman trumpets "truth, justice and the American way" of life, while Christ proclaims, "I am the way, the truth and the life."[6] But are Superman's truth and Christ's truth the same truth?*

Some believers may point out that the Bible warns against taking truth from worldly wise men, scholars, and philosophers who are not invested with the Holy Spirit and therefore are of a profane mind, not the mind of God. They may point to Paul:

Where is the wise man? Where is the scholar? Where is the philosopher of this age? Has not God

---

* Specifically, as we discussed previously, skeptics may question how Christ can claim to be the truth—or as we put it earlier, how all truth is God's truth (see page 30). All truth is God's truth because there is no other truth to draw on apart from what was created in nature, a nature which, as we learned from Paul previously, was created by Christ.[7] Therefore, through creation, God has revealed the truth of himself to all men, even disbelievers, that all people might draw on his truth and reveal it to one another.

made foolish the wisdom of the world? For since in the wisdom of God the world through its wisdom did not know him, God was pleased through the foolishness of what was preached to save those who believe. Jews demand miraculous signs and Greeks look for wisdom, but we preach Christ crucified: a stumbling block to the Jews and foolishness to Gentiles, but to those whom God has called, both Jews and Greeks, Christ the power of God and the wisdom of God.[8]

On the interpretation of this verse, we suggest that what Paul is specifically saying is this: No worldly wisdom, knowledge, or reasoning apart from God could reconcile us to God. In other words, these are wise men, scholars, and philosophers who are in fact not "talking truth": the Jews teach miracles as the Greeks teach wisdom, while both teach in opposition to Christ.

Does this mean that no disbeliever can know and reveal truth? Not at all. Paul also makes it clear God reveals himself through creation: "What may be known about God is plain to them, because God has made it plain to them. For since the creation of the world God's invisible qualities—his eternal power and divine nature—have been clearly seen, being understood from what has been made."[9] This speaks of truth that is revealed to everyone, not only Christians or Jews (even if it is the truth of our God). (The revelation of God

> ## Christ Completes the Truth
>
> Would Christ shun pagans because they do not yet know the full truth of him? We know he has already welcomed those such as the Magi, or Wise Men, at his earthly advent. As G.K. Chesterton recounts, "That truth that is tradition has wisely remembered them almost as unknown quantities, as mysterious as their mysterious and melodious names; Melchior, Caspar, Balthazar. But there came with them all that world of wisdom that had watched the stars in Chaldea and the sun in Persia; and we shall not be wrong if we see in them the same curiosity that moves all the sages.
>
> "They would stand for the same human ideal if their names had really been Confucius or Pythagoras or Plato. They were those who sought not tales but the truth of things; and since their thirst for truth was itself a thirst for God, they also have their reward. But even in order to understand that reward, we must understand that for philosophy as much as mythology, that reward was the completion of the incomplete. Such learned men would doubtless have come, as these learned men did come, to find themselves confirmed in much that was true in their own traditions and right in their own reasoning."

through creation is called *general revelation,* while the additionally needed revelation of Christ is called *special revelation.*)

Such pagan philosophers as the Magi, who learn that their partial truths cannot bridge the gap between man and God, find in Christ first confirmation, then correction, and finally completion of all of their contingent truths.

The Same Truth

Keeping our focus on the mission of service, the warning should be reiterated that to reject what the pagan says simply because a pagan is saying it is putting ourselves in danger of rejecting what God is saying *through* the pagan. This is how Paul can quote from pagans—and if Paul can take that liberty, so can we—because he knows the truth they reveal is God's truth. How can we know which of the things the disbeliever says is truth and which is not? Lest we become latter-day Pilates asking, "What is truth?" of Christ—the very Truth standing in front of him—we should recall that truth can be discerned by a comparison to the standard, God's word, the Holy Writ. In sum, then, it can be said of the shared virtue of "truth" found in the mission statements of Superman and of Christ that it is the *same* truth. And if Superman fights for truth and Christ is the truth, then Superman fights for Christ.

So goes the opening narration of the 1950s *Adventures of Superman* television show with George Reeves, a narration which *Time* magazine describes as a "quasi-liturgical text":

> Strange visitor from another planet, who came to Earth with powers and abilities far beyond those of mortal men. Superman! Who can change the course of mighty rivers, bend steel with his bare hands, and who, disguised as Clark Kent, mild-mannered reporter for a great metropolitan newspaper, fights a never-ending battle for truth, justice, and the American way!

George Reeves, in *Adventures of Superman*. "He was the fatherly Superman in my estimation, mainly because Jack Larson's Jimmy Olsen character was so integral to the plot." (Jerry Ordway, featured writer/artist, *Adventures of Superman* comic book).

Two Important Identities

In regard to the television show's words above, some may find it doubtful that the battle for truth can be waged by a man with a dual identity. However, a closer look will reveal an entirely different understanding of the matter.

Though Superman introduced into comics the now well-known idea of a secret identity, the example existed earlier in the dual life of the God–Man, Jesus Christ. Kal-El chooses to walk among men as Clark and later as Superman much the same as Immanuel chooses to walk among men, first displaying himself as Jesus and later as the Christ.

To the ordinary people of Earth, Clark makes Superman accessible, just as Jesus makes God accessible. The human element makes both relatable. Superman wants to be mild-mannered as Clark for the same reason Christ wants to be meek as Jesus, so that people will not fear him. Yet under the humanity, in each there is a superhuman humility. Gary Engle states of Clark, "He is the epitome of visible invisibility, someone whose extraordinary ordinariness makes him disappear in a crowd." Likewise, John states of Jesus, "The man who was healed had no idea who it was, for Jesus had slipped away into the crowd that was there."[10] Thus the superhero, like the Savior, does not fish around for thanks.

In addition, as also seen in Clark and Superman, the human nature of Jesus gives Christ a personal investment in the well-being of other people, namely his family and friends—and by extension mankind. Drawing a direct line of cause and effect from Jonathan and Martha Kent's love for Clark to Superman's love for humanity, Engle contends that his upbringing influences his destiny:

> This uniquely American hero has two identities, one based on where he comes from in life's journey, one on where he is going....Superman's powers make the hero capable of saving humanity; Kent's total immersion in the American heartland makes him want to do it.

Nor, without their human alter egos, would Christ or Superman have been so warmly embraced. No human friend could have found common ground with their superiority.

A Secret Defense

Paradoxically, for both, the secret identity is a strategic defense. It keeps hidden what is being revealed to the world. The primary way in which Jesus keeps his identity secret is through the use of parables—stories—which keep his message secret. Early on, the parables allow Jesus to continue to be known as Jesus until it is time he becomes known as the Christ. Incredibly, through the parables, those people sincerely seeking spiritual truth find it, and at the same time, those seeking to oppose Christ's work find nothing to accuse him of. In this, the parables provide a way for Christ to illuminate his friends and blind his enemies.

It is as if Jesus' stories also have a dual identity. Illumination occurs when he reveals supernatural truth hidden in everyday stories, uncovering the true meaning of the narrative, the secret identity of the tale. This is a relevant point of application for us. Our modern media culture does a superb job of getting stories out to a vast public, through movies, television shows, songs, books, the Internet, and so on. It is the Christian's task to follow the example of Christ and bring the revelation of what each story means, what spiritual truth is calling out to people from that story. When we see a story that others are drawn to but don't understand its meaning, we should pray for creative discernment. We should ask Christ to "explain everything":

> With many similar parables Jesus spoke the word
> to them, as much as they could understand. He did
> not say anything to them without using a parable.
> But when he was alone with his own disciples, he
> explained everything.[11]

Once we grasp the spiritual truth of the story, we should share that message, so those who are drawn to that story will know why they are drawn there—and to whom.

As a second way to keep his identity secret, Jesus also instructs the people he helps not to tell others he is the Christ. He heals a man with leprosy and tells him, "See that you don't tell this to anyone," because he does not want to be mobbed for being a healer. He stops the demons from naming him the Son of God because he needs time to teach the Jews about his spiritual kingdom before they hail him as a military and political leader. He even raises a little girl from the dead and tells her father, the synagogue ruler, "not to let anyone know about this," because it is too soon for a major confrontation with his enemies, the religious leaders, that might hasten his death and scatter his disciples.[12]

In a parallel pattern, in *Superman: The Movie*, Kal-El maintains his secret identity as Clark Kent according to the plan of his father Jor-El: "You are revealed to the world. Very well. So be it. But you still must keep your secret identity." As Jor-El explains with God-like wisdom, "The reasons are two. First, you cannot serve humanity [twenty-four] hours a day....Your help would be called for endlessly, even for those tasks which human beings could solve for themselves. It is their habit to abuse their resources in such a way." He continues, "Second, your enemies will discover their only way to hurt you: by hurting the people you care for."

Jor-El's second reason is why Gary Engle sees in Superman's dual identity a barometer of his moral purity. Similar to Christ, Superman suffers his secret identity out of love for others:

> The brilliant stroke in the conception of Superman—
> the sine qua non that makes the whole myth
> work—is the fact that he has two identities. The
> myth simply wouldn't work without Clark Kent,
> mild mannered newspaper reporter....Adopting the
> white-bread image of a wimp is first and foremost a
> moral act for the Man of Steel. He does it to protect
> his parents from nefarious sorts who might use them
> to gain an edge over the powerful alien.

Likewise, in *The Great Comic Book Heroes,* Jules Feiffer suggests that the main appeal of Superman rests "in the concept of his alter-ego....Kent was not Superman's true identity....Just the opposite. Clark Kent was the fiction....Superman had only to wake up in the morning to be Superman." Every day he dons the thick-framed glasses and shows up at his workplace, he subjects himself to the small nuisances, petty difficulties, and minor frustrations most others would like to live without. Putting the Superman-in-man duality in messianic terms, Feiffer concludes, "The fellow with the eyeglasses...was a sacrificial disguise, an act of discreet martyrdom."

The Humility of Duality

In the Bible, Paul the apostle, as a man of many identities, offers to us a method of application that Christ—and even Superman—could readily endorse. As Paul presents it,

> To the Jews I became like a Jew, to win the Jews. To those under the law I became like one under the law (though I myself am not under the law), so as to win those under the law. To those not having the law I became like one not having the law....To the weak I became weak, to win the weak. I have become all things to all men so that by all possible means I might save some.[15]

Duality and Disbelief

Concerning Superman's eyeglasses, many a casual critic has noted that, for readers, accepting the glasses as an impenetrable disguise requires a sizable suspension of disbelief.

That loaded word, disbelief, is at the heart of the problem in the biblical precedent as well. Comparable to the way in which his co-workers at the *Daily Planet* cannot recognize Clark as Superman, so the people of his hometown, Nazareth, cannot recognize Jesus as the Christ.[13] Unable to reconcile the carpenter's son they know with the prophesied Savior he is, they reject the idea that one so humble could conceal one so great. In fact, even his own brothers could not believe Jesus was the Christ.[14]

In the Superman comic books, in 1987, this scene of damning denial culminates in *Superman* #2, "The Secret Revealed!" (the second issue of the relaunched comic-book series). When an investigator working for Lex Luthor puts the pieces together and concludes that Superman and Clark Kent are one and the same, Luthor fires her, declaring that no being as supremely powerful as Superman would ever deign to appear as a common man!

This is the same strategy as Christ uses, and following his example, Superman becomes one of us to save all of us. And just as those two figures are willing to lower themselves in order to lift others up, we should not consider ourselves above anyone else, but be willing to bend in order to reach a brother.

A Future Identity

On a larger level, in truth, each of us has a dual identity: One is in the current life, while the other is in the afterlife. As C.S. Lewis reasons,

> Most people, if they had really learned to look into their own hearts, would know that they do want, and want acutely, something that cannot be had in this world. There are all sorts of things in this world that offer to give it to you, but they never quite keep their promise....Creatures are not born with desires unless satisfaction for those desires exists. A baby feels hunger: well, there is such a thing as food. Men feel sexual desire: well, there is such a thing as sex. If I find in myself a desire which no experience in this world can satisfy, the most probable explanation is that I was made for another world.

Indestructible Identity

Bryan Singer, director of *Superman Returns* as well as *X-Men* and *X-Men 2*, comments, "With X-Men, although they had extraordinary powers, they also had physical weaknesses. The suits were for protection as well as costume. Superman is the Man of Steel. Bullets bounce off him, not his suit." Singer sums up, "He's not afraid." And one day neither will we be.

This is the deepest reason why the dual identity of Clark and Superman appeals to us. It confirms for us that we can be more than we appear to be. Or more precisely, that we are less now than we will be later. Either way, it is the optimistic message of the good news—that the Savior can give us a new identity in him and in heaven. "The body that is sown is perishable, it is raised imperishable; it is sown in dishonor, it is raised in glory; it is sown in weakness, it is raised in power."[16] We may look like Clark…but we're really Superman. Or in the biblical version of events, "Just as we have borne the likeness of the earthly man, so shall we bear the likeness of the man from heaven."[17] Like Christ's resurrected body, so will our own bodies be glorious. Those now afflicted with physical, emotional, or mental disabilities can have hope for the future. In our new bodies, we will not need to fear weakness, sickness, or death. In fact, like our comic-book superhero, we will not need to fear any laws of nature,

> for the perishable must clothe itself with the imperishable, and the mortal with immortality. When the perishable has been clothed with the imperishable, and the mortal with immortality, then the saying that is written will come true: "Death has been swallowed up in victory."[18]

Sounds like a pretty super identity.

8

Power in the Blood

* * ✳ * *

*"This is my blood of the covenant, which is
poured out for many."*

JESUS SPEAKING IN MARK 14:24

In heroic literature in general, a hero obtains power in one
of three ways—by active achievement, by passive reception, or
by being born with power. While the first two ways frequently
pertain to human heroes, the last way is most often associated
with gods. This is the way of Superman.

Blessed with Spiritual Strength

Physical strength is one thing. Spiritual strength is another. So
what kind of man is the Man of Steel? The same as he was as a
boy—thanks to the people that reared him. According to *Superman*
#1 (1939), "The love and guidance of his kindly foster-parents
was to become an important factor in the shaping of the boy's

Christopher Reeve on the Superhero

Though talking about Superman, Christopher Reeve could be talking about Christ when he says that what makes him a hero "is not that he has power, but that he has the wisdom and the maturity to use that power wisely. From an acting point of view, that's how I approach the part." So to Reeve—who is "Superman" to hundreds of millions of people worldwide (and whose first name "Christopher" means "Christ-bearer")—this is a hero who has the power not to use his power.

Jesus approaches his role similarly while under siege in the Garden of Gethsemane: "Do you think I cannot call on my Father, and he will at once put at my disposal more than twelve legions of angels? But how then would the Scriptures be fulfilled that say it must happen this way?"[1] In both Superman and Christ, we see a hero whose greatest power is enlightenment.

future." Jonathan and Martha Kent add to Superman's powers "the moral guidance of a Smallville upbringing," as Gary Engle puts it. In the script for *Superman: The Movie*, Mankiewicz describes them as "Christian folk whose morals are as basic as the soil they till." It is the Christian Kents who first instruct the boy Clark to use his great strength "to assist humanity." In this, Superman's code of conduct is the epitome of God's kingdom living. In fact, Superman's attitude perfectly mirrors Christ's beatitudes (blessings based on behaviors). In the Sermon on the Mount, Jesus gives eight characteristics of kingdom living—humility, compassion, meekness, morality, mercy, purity, peacemaking, and perseverance—each of which Superman demonstrates in his daily life (and almost always in *Superman: The Movie*).

Humility. Christ says, "Blessed are the poor in spirit, for theirs is the kingdom of heaven."[2] In *Superman: The Movie*, Clark has this exchange with boss Perry White:

> *Perry:* I've been in this news game forty years, man and boy. And I got to where I am with guts, compassion, elbow grease and something you're sadly lacking in, son.
> *Clark:* Um, humility?
> *Perry:* No! Not humility! You got bags of humility!

Compassion. Christ says, "Blessed are those who mourn, for they will be comforted."[3] Similarly, Superman creator Jerry Siegel explains that his superhero "was very serious about helping people in trouble and distress, because [co-creator] Joe and I felt that very intensely." According to Siegel, the very thing that made Superman stand out from his imitators was "this tremendous feeling of compassion that Joe and I had for the downtrodden." In fact, in one of the earliest newspaper strips, Superman was defined as the "physical marvel who had sworn to devote his existence to helping those in need." Or as Jimmy Olsen (Marc McClure) remarks to Lois in *Superman: The Movie*, "I think he really cares about you." And Lois confirms, "Superman cares about everybody, Jimmy."

Meekness. Christ says, "Blessed are the meek, for they will inherit the earth."[4] Here, we need only evoke the timeless figure of the "mild-mannered" newspaper reporter Clark Kent. Christopher Reeve purposefully portrayed the Man of Steel as modest: "The Superman I wanted to play—the only one I could play—was a low-key one. Very warm, very friendly, very accessible and not at all impressed with himself."

Morality. Christ says, "Blessed are those who hunger and thirst for righteousness, for they will be filled."[5] As noted previously, Superman single-mindedly fights for "truth, justice and the American way." Yet, though he is driven in this righteous pursuit, he does not take matters into his own hands—it is not *his* truth and *his* justice, not like those of a vigilante. Rather, in

---

Saint Superman

The religious aura around *Superman: The Movie* extends even beyond the film. Director Richard Donner remarked, "Somebody asked me, 'Where did you find Reeve?' And I said, 'I didn't find him, God gave him to us.'"

And Christopher Reeve said, "I just took this thing like it was the Bible. Because I felt really in a way the torch had been passed from previous generations of actors and readers who had loved Superman. So I felt that during the '70s and the '80s I was the temporary custodian of a part that is an essential piece of American mythology."

However, Reeve was only human, and he also felt the weight of the part: "Religious figures have called me up and asked if I'm aware of the responsibilities of being a contemporary Christ figure. Hey, I'm an actor from New Jersey; I can't be responsible for that." Neither the clergymen nor Reeve needed to be so concerned. As an actor, he was not Jesus any more than he was Superman. Yet as a symbol, he was undeniably both.

good conscience, he works with law enforcers to direct criminals through the court system.

Just as Jesus comes not to abolish the law but to fulfill it,[6] so does Superman. In the shooting script for *Superman: The Movie,* when Superman delivers Luthor to prison, the warden beams and declares, "This country is safe again, Superman—thanks to you." To which the hero replies, "And you, Warden. And the fireman, the doctor, the teacher, the clergyman—the cop on the beat....We're all on the same team."

Mercy. Christ says, "Blessed are the merciful, for they will be shown mercy."[7] In the movie, Clark asks his employer to send half of his salary on a weekly basis to a certain address. While Lois first guesses that this is for Clark's bookie, she later jokes that Clark is sending money home to his "gray-haired old mother."

"Actually, she's silver-haired," Clark corrects her. Impressed with this sacrificial act of mercy, Lois asks if there are any more at home like him.

Purity. Christ says, "Blessed are the pure in heart, for they will see God."[8] In the movie, during the rooftop interview, when Lois becomes incredulous that Superman could be so good, she exclaims, "I don't believe this!" "Lois," Superman calls with a kind smile and locks eyes with her, "I never lie." Likewise, to highlight the purity of the character, Reeve plays Superman as somebody "you can invite home for dinner...someone you can introduce your parents to."

Peacemaking. Christ says, "Blessed are the peacemakers, for they will be called sons of God."[9] In *Superman: The Movie,* Jor-El the father indicates that peace is the ultimate goal of Kal-El his son:

> You are superior to others. You can only become
> inferior by setting yourself above them. Lead by
> inspiration. Let your actions and ideals become a
> touchstone against which mankind may learn how

to serve the common good. While it is forbidden for you to interfere with human history itself, your leadership can stir others to their own capacity for moral betterment.

Perseverance. Christ says, "Blessed are those who are persecuted because of righteousness, for theirs is the kingdom of heaven."[10] For Superman, the fight for "truth, justice and the American way" is, after all, "a never-ending battle."

A Refreshing Message

As screenwriter Mankiewicz confirms of *Superman: The Movie,* "What we are giving people is the Christian message: that we should be honest, love one another, and be for the underdog." Indeed, as Kozlovic points out, throughout the movie (as well as in other venues), Superman is

> shown as a man that honours his parents, treats his coworkers with respect, is sexually chaste as far as romance is concerned, and genuinely cares about the welfare and safety of others....It is refreshing to spend time in a world where sin has consequences, evildoers are punished, good is rewarded, and traditional moral values are seen as good and honorable.

And, as indicated before, it is a world in which the hero is super both spiritually and physically. In Christ and Superman, we find morals backed up by muscles, powers rested on principles—a combination that makes the ethical behavior of either all the more admirable because it comes from a strength of character rather than a position of weakness. As Michael Mautner observes, though Clark Kent is humiliated at times, Superman has no need of personal vengeance because "Superman is a paragon of virtue; he acts mostly on altruistic motives." Superman manhandles criminals to satisfy the audience's demands for justice, just as Christ will judge evildoers to—among other reasons—satisfy the Christian demands

Powers That Attract

The superpowers of Superman embody symbolic references to the miraculous powers of Christ—which is why the powers appeal to us.

- Superman gets his powers from the *sun* (his body stores solar energy), forging a phonetic link to Christ, who is the Son—and the one we get *our* power from.

- Both Superman and Christ possess superhuman strength: Superman physically, Christ spiritually. And we want a Savior strong enough to overcome all opposition.

- Superman has X-ray vision; and nothing is hidden from God's sight. And we long to have nothing to hide, nothing to fear being exposed.

- Superman has heat vision; the resurrected Christ has eyes like blazing fire. And we are desperate for a purifying fire, one that can burn away our evil desires.

- Superman has superhearing; God hears prayers before they are said. And we need our Savior to hear us whenever, from wherever, however or for whatever we call!

- Superman is "faster than a speeding bullet"; Christ heals an absent son the instant his father professes faith. And we want a Savior who can react immediately.

- Superman flies up, up, and away, just as Christ ascends into the heavens. And we yearn to join God above it all.[11]

for justice. An excellent example of this occurs near the end of *Superman II*. Earlier in the story, a de-powered Clark suffers a brutal beating in a roadside diner at the hands of a bully. We feel for Clark—our desire for justice is aroused. Thus, near the end of the movie—significantly, after Clark has regained his super strength and saved the whole world—he returns to the diner to serve the bully his just deserts—for us.

Divine Virtues

Recently in the canon, Superman has manifested two powers that appear to be borrowed directly from the unique, proprietary powers of Christ: one of blood, the other of spirit. Given *Smallville*'s penchant for explicit Christic imagery, it should come as only a small shock that both of these powers are demonstrated over the same story arc.

Sanguinary Cures

That storyline, which spans an epic 35 episodes, begins in "Fever" (#37) when Clark inhales spores of kryptonite, loses his strength, and collapses. In his powerless state, his blood is taken and put under the microscope. It confounds the attending physician. After Clark recovers, the doctor, Helen Bryce, keeps an unmarked vial of the unusual blood in her office. Because the doctor is in a relationship with Lex Luthor, the curious nature of the mysterious blood comes to his attention. Eventually, the vial winds up in the hands of Lex's father, Lionel Luthor (John Glover), a character created for the television show. Lionel, dying of liver disease and driven to find a cure, experiments with the blood in hopes of developing a serum, which he tests on the recently expired bodies of liver disease victims—to astonishing effect. As one LuthorCorp scientist states, the platelets in the blood "have the remarkable ability to revivify necrotic tissue"—that is, this blood has the power to raise the dead to life. Obviously, this notion has its origin in the blood of Jesus, shed as a sacrifice for our sins to redeem us from an eternal death for an eternal life with him.[12]

As the story arc continues, in an episode significantly entitled "Resurrection" (#59), while Jonathan Kent is in the hospital for heart surgery, Clark learns that people can be saved by his blood. Then he and his parents have an exchange that is specific to them yet reverberates with Christic echoes:

> *Clark:* I think Lionel Luthor has found a way to use my blood to bring people back to life. If my blood can save lives, maybe I should come forward. What if there's something inside of me that can repair Dad's heart, permanently?
>
> *Jonathan:* Clark, your mother and I both know that you are going to save a lot of lives in this world. Even more than you have any idea.
>
> *Clark:* The only life I'm interested in saving is yours.
>
> *Jonathan:* You do. You save my life every day that you're with us. And we wouldn't trade that for a single moment without you.*

---

* Just in case the connection to the lifesaving blood of the Lamb remains unnoticed, within the boxed set of *Smallville—The Complete Third Season,* the creators of the DVD chapter menu for this episode provide a sign. The chapter that contains this discussion between Clark and his father bears the title "Power in the Blood," which is borrowed from the renowned hymn "There Is Power in the Blood," a song of praise for the lifesaving blood of the Lamb.

Life in the Spirit

Having depicted one of the unique, proprietary powers of Christ in Clark's blood, *Smallville* goes on to demonstrate the same in Clark's spirit. The long-running storyline reaches a conclusion of sorts in "Transference" (#72), when Lionel, now in jail on murder charges and still ailing with terminal liver disease, calls Lex to the prison ostensibly to make amends. However, the elder Luthor harbors a cruel plan to touch Lex with a strange stone that will transfer his spirit into Lex's body, leaving Lex's spirit in Lionel's diseased body to die in prison. Luckily for Lex, the stone emits a high-pitched ring that reaches the ears of Clark, who rushes in and stops Lionel from touching Lex with it. Unfortunately for Clark, Lionel touches him with the stone instead, and Lionel's spirit transfers into Clark's body while, more importantly to the payoff of this episode, the spirit of Clark is invested into Lionel's sickened body.

Subsequently, Clark meets Lionel's conspicuous cellmate, a mathematician "looking for hidden patterns in the Dead Sea Scrolls" who, after being framed for stealing, was conveniently assigned to Luthor's cell and informed Luthor of the strange stone. After a few days, in which Clark unjustly suffers the oppressions of prison and Lionel wreaks havoc in the superteenager's life, Lionel ("Lion-El"?) learns he must kill his old body to make the transfer permanent. But because Clark is ready for him, when Lionel comes for Clark, Clark touches Lionel with the stone, and Clark's spirit returns to his original body while Lionel's spirit does the same.

At that moment, something occurs, the meaning of which is not made clear until four episodes later. When Lionel's spirit returns to his body, he drops to the floor, his face gaunt and jaundiced. Suddenly vibrant color returns to his cheeks, and he stares wide-eyed at a figure above. Through a haze made white by the overhead lights, we see the shadowy silhouette of the restored Clark looking down on Lionel, a benevolent victor checking over his fallen opponent. Then, in a flash of superspeed, Clark is gone, leaving Lionel gaping after.

A little later in the same episode, in the prison infirmary, Lionel receives the good news (*Smallville*'s allegorical Good News)—his liver disease has been miraculously healed. Testifies the doctor, "It's the closest thing to a miracle I've ever seen." Not only that, but Lionel, who cannot remember the events of the past week, is nevertheless moved to share his witness, inasmuch as he understands it. "I just know that something here, inside of me, has changed—profoundly. I'm not the same man." Thus, symbolic of the powers of the Holy Spirit of God,[13] the superspirit of Clark also has the ability to heal a sinful man both physically and spiritually.

Four episodes later, in "Scare" (#76), the meaning of Lionel's earlier engagement with the haloed silhouette of Clark becomes apparent when the prison warden comes to see Luthor, a new man, a better man, one now pure in spirit, thought, and deed. In the discussion that follows, Warden Anita Stone makes a key comparison of her prisoner to a scriptural figure, which Lionel affirms in overtly religious language.

> *Warden Stone:* I hope I didn't separate you from your flock.
> *Lionel:* I understand your cynicism, Warden Stone. But I assure you I truly am a changed man.
> *Warden Stone:* Or maybe just a smart one. Ever since you proclaimed this sudden conversion to our resident Saint Paul, there hasn't been a single attempt on your life.
> *Lionel:* I want only to be of help to others. What is the value of my sinful life, unless I use it as an example to shepherd fellow sinners? To lead them away from the allure of hedonism and mistrust and greed? To follow a better way?

Here we can refer to the encounter in which the sinner Saul becomes the original "Saint Paul":

> As he neared Damascus on his journey, suddenly a
> light from heaven flashed around him. He fell to
> the ground and heard a voice say to him, "Saul, Saul,
> why do you persecute me?" "Who are you, Lord?"
> Saul asked. "I am Jesus, whom you are persecuting,"
> he replied. "Now get up and go into the city, and
> you will be told what you must do."[14]

With Lionel newly paired to Saul/Paul, the understanding of his
mysterious, shadowy meeting with Clark, our established Christ
figure, is made amazingly unmistakable. For a while at least,
Superman gains an apostle.

9

TRUE BLUE

*   *   ✳   *   *

"If I only touch his cloak, I will be healed."

A WOMAN IN NEED OF HEALING,
SPEAKING IN MATTHEW 9:21

As *Superman Returns* director Bryan Singer pointed out earlier, the elemental nature of Superman's powers is highlighted by his costume (see sidebar on page 82). More even than his powers, his blue suit, red cape, and especially yellow "S" shield have become the most readily identifiable elements of the Superman iconography. Around the globe, few other symbols, religious or otherwise, are so universally recognized as the "S" shield. Singer makes this point on the impact of the "S" in the stylized triangle—while also revealing his recognition of associations between Superman and Christ:

It's an icon that surpasses probably any comic icon and most icons that exist in popular culture. I guarantee you take the cross and the "S" into the jungle and you will have 50/50 recognition.

*   *   ✳   *   *

While the suit of Superman hasn't changed much—still blue body, red cape, "S" on chest—the story of how the costume came to be certainly has. Although this is not widely known, originally, in a comic from the summer of 1940, Superman creates the uniform himself, right down to the fabric, describing the costume as "constructed of a cloth I invented myself which is immune to the most powerful forces!"

In 1952, with the television premiere of *Adventures of Superman,* the version that would become canon arises when Ma Kent makes the blue, yellow, and red suit out of the three colorful blankets in which the interplanetary infant arrived. In a cute back story to this version, in the July 1961 *Superman* #146, Martha is first compelled to weave the Kryptonian blankets into an indestructible playsuit because the supertoddler keeps annihilating his Earth clothes. Equally clever, to complete the costume, in the winter 1963 *Superman Annual* #8, when Clark comes of age and Ma reworks the material into the celebrated uniform, "the young Superman used 'strips of rubber padding' salvaged from the wreckage of his rocket to fashion a pair of bright red boots, while a yellow strip, also salvaged from the rocket, became his belt," as Michael Fleisher describes.

Primary Colors

Nevertheless, it still depends on who you ask as to whether the suit is inherently indestructible, becomes so under the Earth's yellow sunrays, or is actually ordinary Earth material that achieves invulnerability by virtue of Superman's bioelectric aura. Inventive storytelling aside, Superman's suit has proven appealing due to the uses of color and symbol incorporated into the uniform. These colors and symbols carry meaning that we recognize consciously or unconsciously, because they embody certain religious signifiers.

Blue, yellow, and red are the primary colors. They cannot be formed by any combination of other colors; instead, all other colors are derived from them. They are a virtual Trinity of the color set, and their meanings in the Bible are noteworthy:

* *Blue—the color of Superman's bodysuit—is the color of God or, alternately, of faith.* As the Lord instructs Moses, "Throughout the generations to come you are to make tassels on the corners of your garments, with a blue cord on each tassel. You will have these tassels to look at and so you will remember all the commands of the LORD." Blue is also the color of the sky or heaven and thus is associated with Christ who has "come down from heaven not to do my will but to do the will of him who sent me."[1]

* *Yellow—the hue of Superman's "S" shield and belt—is the color of glory, or alternately of hope as symbolized by gold.* Gold is one of three gifts given to Jesus after his birth.[2] Gold is in the prophecy of the future reign of Christ on earth: "'The silver is mine and the gold is mine,' declares the LORD Almighty. 'The glory of this present house will be greater than the glory of the former house.'" And gold is in the crown on Christ at Judgment as he harvests Christians for their reward: "I looked, and there before me was a white cloud, and seated on the cloud was one 'like a son of man' with a crown of gold on his head and a sharp sickle in his hand."[3]

* *Red—the color of Superman's cape, boots, shorts, and "S"—can be seen as the color of love, or alternately of blood,* as exemplified in the blood Jesus shed out of love for us, "him who loves us and has freed us from our sins by his blood."[4]

Superman an Angel Figure?

An alternative interpretation of Superman–as an angel figure–is supported by intriguing similarities in the actions of the world's greatest superhero and one of the heavenly host. Angels patrol the earth, protect the helpless, defend the innocent, serve the good, carry out justice, and fight the forces of evil[6]–as does the Man of Steel.

Gary Engle concludes, noting a phenomenon in Superman's country of origin that also applies to the rest of the world, "In America, cultural icons that manage to tap the national religious spirit are of necessity secular on the surface and sufficiently generalized to incorporate the diversity of American religious traditions. Superman doesn't have to be seen as an angel to be appreciated, but in the absence of a tradition of national religious iconography, he can serve as a safe, nonsectarian focus for essentially religious sentiments, particularly among the young."

Given these three delineations in biblical color symbolism, if blue means faith, yellow means hope, and red means love, then we find on Superman a tricolor uniform the apostle Paul would approve of. "These three remain: faith, hope and love. But the greatest of these is love."[5]

Angelic Cape?

The cape of Superman, when considered on its own, presents a compelling parallel in religious symbolism. Moreover, it was the first cape of its kind. As Gary Engle recounts,

It wasn't the cape of Victorian melodrama and adventure fiction, the kind worn with a clasp around the neck. In fact, one is hard-pressed to find any precedent in popular culture for the kind of cape Superman wears. His emerges in a seamless line from either side of the front yoke of his tunic. It is a veritable growth from behind his pectorals and hangs, when he stands at ease, in a line that doesn't so much drape his shoulders as stand apart from them and echo their curve, like an angel's wings.

Shield and Symbol

Still, above all other aspects of the costume, the focal point of the Superman suit remains the "S" on his chest. Co-creator and illustrator Shuster gives this account:

Jerry Siegel and I came up with the "S" insignia—we

discussed it in detail. We said, "Let's put something on the front of the costume." From the beginning we wanted to somehow use the first letter of the character's name. We thought S was perfect. After we came up with it, we kiddingly said, "Well, it's the first letter of Siegel and Shuster."

Shuster then cites his inspiration for the frame surrounding the "S," stating, "Initially I made it like a shield, a fancy little triangle with curves at the top. I had a heraldic crest in the back of my mind."*

As does the color scheme, the shapes in the "S" shield also have special meanings. There are two forms to note: the stylized triangle, and the "S" itself. On the importance of the triangle, scholar Robert Styer elucidates, "Although everyone agrees that physical symbols cannot hope to encompass truths as deep as the Trinity, the human mind seems to seek immanent [immediately present] representations of transcendent truth." He goes on to remind us,

> From the early centuries of the church variations of a triangle have symbolized the Trinity. The equilateral triangle is a powerful picture of the coequal nature of the three persons. It stresses the distinctions, the "is not" doctrine, of the three persons by the maximal separation of the vertices. Many triangular images have been used to symbolize the Trinity.

One of the most prominent triangular representations of God is the Star of David (in Hebrew, *magen Dawid*, literally, "shield

---

* The *heraldic crest* is the badge of the herald, a reference that offers an interesting implication when seen through our Christ-colored glasses. It recasts Superman into yet another biblical role. The herald announces someone to come. The herald supports or advocates; he is a spokesman or forerunner. So of whom is Superman the herald, of whom is he the forerunner? In Bible times, the original forerunner of Jesus is John the Baptist, who—like Superman to the second coming—might also be called the herald of Christ.

of David"). This symbol features two interlocking triangles, one pointed up, the position of man pointing up toward God, and the other pointed down, the position of God pointing down toward man. This second position, of God pointing down toward man, is the position of the triangle in the shield of Superman.

The Creation of the "S"

As for the "S" on Superman's chest, similar to the construction of the suit itself, a few different versions of events exist for how it got there. First, in the January 1945 *More Fun Comics* #101, the young Superboy himself chooses the "S" for the front of his junior-sized super suit. Later, as referenced before, in the 1952 pilot episode of *Adventures of Superman,* the multitalented Ma Kent not only makes the costume but also, one assumes, creates the soon-to-be-famous "S" shield while she is at it.

In the October 1979 *Action Comics* #500, Pa Kent designs the "S" emblem, which allows him, alongside Ma, to also have a hand in crafting the supersuit. Fleshing out this version, in the 1984 *Superman Annual* #10, Pa beholds a vision of the "S" shield in a dream, as if by divine revelation. This is one scene of an immense mosaic storyline that spans numerous issues and records how, since the beginning of the universe, godlike beings have guided the planet Krypton, the race of Kryptonians, and finally the House of El to give rise to one perfect savior, solidifying for many readers what one commentator describes as the image of Superman as a "Christ-like force in the universe."

In 1987, when the *Man of Steel* comic-book miniseries officially revamped the

A Family Crest

In *Superman: The Movie,* the "S" stands for "El." It isn't even an "S," but rather a Kryptonian family crest (a concept later supported by *Smallville* and *Superman Returns*), made apparent by its appearance on Jor-El's chest at the first of the film.

Creative consultant Tom Mankiewicz explained, "You'll see, by the way, that Marlon Brando [Jor-El] has an 'S' on his chest. Because one of the great riddles we tried to figure out was why Superman has an 'S' on his chest. Because it obviously stands for 'Superman' but he wasn't called 'Superman' till he got this. So why does he have an 'S' on his chest? So we decided to give everyone [on Krypton] a family crest with a different letter, which didn't really exist in the comic books."

origin story, once again, Clark himself creates the "S" logo. Then, in the 1999 comic-book miniseries *The Kents*, another intriguing element is added to the mythology of the "S" that creates new connections to the imagery of Christ.

Within this story, after Clark has been Superman in Metropolis for years, Jonathan uncovers a strongbox belonging to the first Kents to settle in Kansas, in the 1800s. Along with a collection of letters and journals, incredibly, Jonathan finds a blue blanket featuring a yellow stylized triangle around a red S-shaped form. The blanket is an Iroquois healing cover, and the S form is a snake, an animal totem that sheds its skin in a symbolic act of rebirth and restoration.

Healing in the "S"

In the Bible, the snake as a symbol of healing is originated in a story arc spanning 1500 years and bridging that distance from the earlier books of the Old Testament into the New. As the Israelites wandered in the desert,

> they spoke against God and against Moses, and said, "Why have you brought us up out of Egypt to die in the desert? There is no bread! There is no water! And we detest this miserable food!" Then the LORD sent venomous snakes among them; they bit the people and many Israelites died. The people came to Moses and said, "We sinned when we spoke against the LORD and against you. Pray that the LORD will take the snakes away from us." So Moses prayed for the people. The LORD said to Moses, "Make a snake and put it up on a pole; anyone who is bitten can look at it and live." So Moses made a bronze snake and put it up on a pole. Then when anyone was bitten by a snake and looked at the bronze snake, he lived.[7]

Seven hundred years later, King Hezekiah of Israel makes a startling discovery, which he deals with in an equally startling way. Upon finding a group of Israelites unfaithful to God bowing down to a certain snake statue, he "broke into pieces the bronze snake Moses had made, for up to that time the Israelites had been burning incense to it."[8] Hence, the healing snake, having become a relic to worship rather than a reminder of whom to worship, lies smashed at the feet of a godly king—and remains there for 700 more years until the story concludes in the New Testament book of John—with a surprising declaration from Christ himself.

In a conversation on being born again, Jesus declares, "Just as Moses lifted up the snake in the desert, so the Son of Man must be lifted up, that everyone who believes in him may have eternal life."[9] Thus, Christ makes whole again this symbol of healing when he compares himself to the snake as an emblem of restoration, redemption, and reconciliation both physical and spiritual.

Likewise, on the resemblance of the Superman "S" shield to the Iroquois snake symbol, Scott Beatty writes, "Superman's emblem evokes the power to heal. It is recognized everywhere on Earth…and even beyond Kal-El's adopted world!" While we'll have to take his word on that last part, in principle we couldn't agree more. The strikingly similar appearance and meaning of the "S" shield and the snake symbol indicates one common source for both, something larger or higher at work…a God-inspired use of images.

Hope in the "S"

Finally, the 2002 comic-book miniseries *Superman: Birthright* offers a culmination of the more prominent versions of how the "S" came into being when it reveals that the shield is both the family crest—and more than the family crest. As Clark recounts in the story,

> At first, I thought it was a family crest of some sort—but if it was, it certainly came to mean more than that to these people. Wars were fought over it. Entire cities were built on it. Over the course of time,

it became a…promise. A sign of people fighting to
make a better world. A symbol of hope.

Indeed, as a trinitarian symbol of God, healing, and now hope,
the "S" shield on the chest serves well as a symbolic stand-in for
the cross worn around the neck.

10

A SUPER MAN

* * ✳ * *

"But what about you," he asked.
"Who do you say I am?"

JESUS, IN MARK 8:29

"Did you ever hear of Superman?" the newspaper editor barks at his reporter, assigning the story to a startled Clark Kent—and thus, in *Action Comics* #1, the "Chief" becomes the first person to ever utter the hero's title (apparently, fate told him). Later, in a Superboy story, it seems Superman names himself. In *More Fun Comics* #101, when Superboy chooses the "S," he picks the letter "not only to stand for Superboy, and later Superman—it will also mean Saving lives, Stopping crime, and giving Super-aid wherever it's needed!" In *The Adventures of Superman*, the new label is given him by the first person he rescues who calls him "this…super man." Finally—as the version the Superman canon in general accepts—in *Superman: The Movie*, after our superhero takes her on a nighttime flight, it is Lois Lane who gives him the immortal name: "What a super man…"

A Dark Origin

Yet, in reality, the term *Superman* was not original with Superman. Neither was the name original with Siegel and Shuster. Rather, the name was created by German philosopher Friedrich Nietzsche in 1883. He used the name to describe a man who overcame human limitations, including the confining concepts of good and evil, a man such as Julius Caesar or Napoleon Bonaparte. His word *Übermensch* was translated as "overman" or, more popularly received, "superman." *Smallville* has fun with this in the pilot episode when Lana notices Clark carries a Nietzsche schoolbook:

> *Lana:* Nietzsche. Didn't realize you had a dark side, Clark.
> *Clark:* Doesn't everybody?
> *Lana:* Yeah, I guess so. So which are you, man or superman?
> *Clark:* I haven't figured it out yet.

The term *superman* is taken from a work entitled *Thus Spake Zarathustra*, in which Nietzsche infamously proclaimed "God is dead." Though Nietzsche's father was a Lutheran minister, he died when his son was five, and Nietzsche gravitated toward philosophy later in life, viewing Christianity as a stumbling block to greatness. *Zarathustra* is a series of dialogues loosely structured after the synoptic gospels (Matthew, Mark, and Luke). When Nietzsche announced God's death, he was actually saying *belief* in God was dead. Therefore, a man would have to become his own God—a superman. To do this, the worthy one would separate himself from the crowd, rise above the

Nietzsche's Notes

The link to Nietzsche was made musically in *Superman II* in an "imaginative stroke by arranger Ken Thorne at the beginning [of the film when he] inverts one of John Williams' musical motifs and turns it into a direct quote from Richard Strauss' *Also Sprach Zarathustra*," as Anton Kozlovic points out.

great unwashed, and eventually command the masses. Later, beginning in the 1920s Hitler and his followers distorted the idea of the superman to justify their murderous designs for an "Aryan nation."

From Nietzsche, the term trickled down into science-fiction literature, where writers used the label "superman" to describe jet-packed, helmeted heroes or powerful, often otherworldly villains. This is where Siegel and Shuster became familiar with the title. However, as Les Daniels notes of Jerry Siegel, "the determination of this young Jewish-American to find a personality that matched the word was finally so successful that his concept is remembered today by hundreds of millions who may barely know who Nietzsche is." Of course, as detailed previously, the "personality that matched the word" matched the personality of Christ.

In fact, according to Michael Mautner,

> Nietzsche was probably rolling over in his grave, for the Man of Tomorrow was the antithesis of his "superman." Greatness personified, he surrendered himself willingly to the people, the swarms of "flies," and fought for them with joy. The Nazis, not surprisingly, attacked the character, pointing to Siegel's Jewish roots as "proof" that Superman was a "poisonous" influence on American youth.

Although Nietzsche would doubtless disagree, the symbolism of God-as-man still becomes concrete in one figure—and it is neither Caesar nor Napoleon. Rather, the "supermen" of both Nietzsche and Siegel find common ground in this key facet: Both are Christ figures. Between the two, over the man of will, we'll take the Man of Steel.

Rubbing Shoulders with Humanity

"I want the name of this flying what-cha-ma-call-it to go with the *Daily Planet* like bacon and eggs, franks and beans, death and taxes, politics and corruption," the newspaper editor barks again (although by the time of *Superman: the Movie,* the Chief

Superman's Music

One other element, as introduced in *Superman: The Movie*, has become an intrinsic mark of Superman–his music. Rarely has such a strong association been made between a character and his musical theme. According to one reviewer, the three climactic notes of the theme are "melodically arranged in such a way that the listener is almost compelled to sing the word 'Superman' as if it were a lyric."

Director Richard Donner recalls the day composer John Williams scored the opening credits with these remarks: "When the word Superman came up on the screen, he orchestrated the word. I've never heard it done in my life. But you can hear the music say 'SU-PER-MAN.' He actually said the word with the music. And I just couldn't believe it."

Another critic commented with near religious reverence on the "majestic piece of music, whose strains seem to emanate from some wellspring of greatness far away, and which gathers energy and power so quickly that the mind almost cannot keep up with it." Maestro Williams himself explains the purpose of the music in terms of its spiritual application: "There's a lot of mythology in it [the story] and this mythological/mystical reach into the soul, into our inner life, was the role of the music." Superman is so linked with his theme that nearly 30 years after the score was first recorded (and after a handful of special appearances on *Smallville*), the piece of music reappears once again as the Superman theme in *Superman Returns*.

has a name: Perry White—played by Jackie Cooper.) "Now listen to me. I tell you, boys and girls, whichever one of you gets it out of him, is going to wind up with the single most important interview since..." Perry searches for an example before finding one of biblical proportions, "...God talked to Moses!" (And the judges will accept that answer!)

Aside from Perry (the prophet— see next page), the *Daily Planet* office offers other Christic parallels. Originally, Clark has a very practical purpose for coming to work at the newspaper: The crime reports keep him informed on the seamier side of the city. So he states in a December 1949 issue, "As a reporter, I have a hundred underworld and police contacts that make it easier for Superman to fight crime!" In a similar vein, Christ spends so much time with sinners that he is accused of being one: "The Son of man came eating and drinking, and they say, 'Here is a glutton and a drunkard, a friend of tax collectors and "sinners."' But wisdom is proved right by her actions."[1]

In addition, both Clark and Christ work with writers who influence the culture. As Kozlovic reminds us, "Just as Clark Kent rubbed shoulders with his journalist peers who reported upon the activities of Superman, Jesus kept company with Matthew and John, the

Gospel writers who reported upon the activities of the Messiah." Indeed, as a chronicle of a Savior, the *Daily Planet* resembles a Gospel. (At first, the *Daily Planet* was the *Daily Star*, recalling the Star of Bethlehem, which also heralds a hero.)

Furthermore, the close associates of Clark mirror the figures closest to Christ and thereby highlight Superman's messianic identity. Editor Perry White can be seen as John the Baptist, the prophet devoted to revealing the Savior. Biblically, his last name, "White," as noted before, signifies holiness.[2] Cub reporter Jimmy Olsen can be seen as a combined representation of the apostles. His full name is actually James Bartholomew Olsen; in "James" and "Bartholomew," he bears the names of three apostles: James son of Zebedee, James son of Alphaeus, and Bartholomew.

Most notably, girl reporter Lois Lane can be seen as Mary Magdalene, a prominent woman in Christ's circle of friends. Notice the alliteration in the name Lois Lane, the repetition of the same first letter, which seems borrowed from the name Mary Magdalene.*

Friend and Lover?

Of Superman's girlfriend, Kozlovic reports, "Sarah Kozloff argued that Lois Lane...'roughly parallels Mary Magdalene...the prostitute reformed and converted by Jesus who becomes one of his most faithful followers...Lois Lane...assumes the role of Superman's most devoted and most favoured disciple, and while she is not presented as a prostitute...she is repeatedly associated with sex." In her initial interview with Superman, first she asks if he has a wife or girlfriend, next she asks how big he is (instead of how tall), then she asks him to use X-ray vision to tell the color of her underpants. He tells her "pink," and later she asks if he likes "pink." The most blatant point of the connection between Lois and sex is reached in the title of her article: "I Spent the Night with Superman."

Nevertheless, it is a misinterpretation of the Bible that Mary Magdalene is a prostitute. (This widespread misperception probably started with a sermon by Pope Gregory I in the year 591, and the Vatican officially rejected this idea in 1969.) While Scripture tells us Jesus cast seven demons out of her,[4] it does not explicitly say she is a prostitute. (With these exact same stipulations, we'll beat fans of the Apocrypha to the punch by acknowledging that the subsequent romance which develops between Lois and Superman echoes "the many extra-canonical stories of Mary Magdalene being the secret lover of Jesus.")

---

* From biblical times, the name *Lois* means "more desirable." *Lane*, as is obvious, means "narrow path." Put together, "Lois Lane" connotes a "more desirable narrow path," biblically resonant with Christianity: "Small is the gate and narrow the road that leads to life, and only a few find it."[3]

The Messiah for Lois

As Lois interacts with Superman in the movie, she also reflects the roles of biblical figures who interact with Christ besides Mary Magdalene. In the nighttime flight that follows the interview, Lois symbolically assumes the place of the apostle Peter. As indicated earlier, Superman's ability to fly through the air mirrors Christ's ability to walk on water. Just as Christ invites Peter to walk with him, Superman invites Lois to fly with him. "Then Peter got down out of the boat, walked on the water and came toward Jesus."[5]

At one point during the flight, Lois inches her grasp out along Superman's arm until only their fingers are touching. The image of the two hands touching, the powerful and the frail, the immortal and the mortal, seems reminiscent of the hands of God and Adam in the painting on the ceiling of the Sistine Chapel, the "image of divinity meeting humanity as most famously represented in Michelangelo's *The Creation of Adam*," as Kozlovic observes. Memorably, a little later, Lois thinks to herself, "Here I am…holding hands with a god."

And, in a nearly identical reflection of the scriptural account, just as Peter loses his focus on Christ and begins to sink through the water, Lois loses touch with Superman and begins to fall through the air. "When he saw the wind, he was afraid and, beginning to sink, cried out, 'Lord, save me!'" In both cases, however, the leader catches his follower; as Christ reaches down to Peter, Superman swoops down to Lois. "Immediately, Jesus reached out his hand and caught him. 'You of little faith,' he said, 'Why did you doubt?'"[6] Toward the end of the flight, a white dove flutters past the smiling couple. In the Bible, as mentioned earlier, the dove is the symbol of God's Holy Spirit descending to show approval, an emblem of peace and salvation.[7]

For one very significant moment, Lois also recalls the apostle Thomas, though the sign is reversed. In *Superman II*, when Clark burns his hand in a fire, Lois examines his hand, finds no mark, and thereafter believes Clark is Superman. This breaks a cardinal rule in the Superman story, a principle that must be reestablished before the end of the movie. It is intriguing that, out of all the ways his identity could have been confirmed, all of the superpowers she could have secretly witnessed to bring about the "great reveal," it all comes down to an inspection of the hero's hand, as it did for doubting Thomas. However, whereas Lois looks to find no mark, Thomas wants only to *see* a mark. Of the resurrected Savior, Thomas declares, "Unless I see the nail marks in his hands and put my finger where the nails were...I will not believe it."[8] A week later, Jesus reappears, Thomas examines his hands to find the marks, and thereafter believes that Jesus is the risen Christ.

A Miracle for Lois

Indeed, it is Lois that gives Superman occasion for one of his greatest and most Christlike feats—one which demonstrates his complete control over the physical world.* In *Superman: The Movie*, at the height of the film, Superman attempts to redirect into space one of two nuclear missiles launched by Lex Luthor. Meanwhile, as Lois drives along a desert backroad, the second nuclear missile strikes the San Andreas Fault, causing an earthquake that rips apart the countryside.

During the aftershocks, unable to stop for fuel, Lois drives until her car stalls, the gas tank empty. Suddenly, a fissure appears, racing up behind her car. The cracking earth opens under the car, and she slides into the gaping crevasse. Dirt pours in through the windows, covering her arms, shoulders, and finally her face. The fissure begins to close, entombing her; she stops moving; more dirt pours in.

Finally, Superman arrives. He lifts the car out, rips the door off, and removes Lois from the front seat. She is not breathing, having suffocated to death. He weeps, as did Christ at the death

---

* Interestingly, since *Superman: The Movie* and *Superman II* were written together, a part of this sequence was first planned as the ending to *Superman II*—to make Lois forget she knew Clark was Superman. However, near the end of production on the first film, it was moved here to give the ending more emotional resonance.

of Lazarus.[9] Slowly, his sorrow turns to anger, which turns to rage. With a scream, he launches himself into the heavens. He streaks through the atmosphere, ignoring the echoing objection of Jor-El (oddly antagonistic and out of character), "It is forbidden for you to interfere with human history," following instead the reverberating advice of Jonathan—"You are here for a reason." Almost immediately, Superman has completed his first circle of the Earth. He continues around a second, a third, a fourth time. He is flying counter to its rotation. He strains to fly faster, ever faster.

Incredibly, the rotation of the Earth slows, then stops, then begins to go backward. Time follows suit. We see the disastrous events happening in reverse. A landslide rolls uphill. A flood flows upstream. A cracked dam reseals. Lois's car rises out of the ground.

Above the Earth, Superman returns the world to its proper rotation. Moments later, when he touches down next to her, Lois is sitting in her stalled car, alive and well, though a little perturbed at Superman for not getting there sooner. Kozlovic notes that "when he resurrected Lois, he acted like Jesus who brought back from the dead the ruler's daughter…the only son of the widowed mother…and Lazarus."[10]

*   *   ✳   *   *

Thus, at the end of the end of the mission story and the beginning of the destiny story, it's clear Superman, like Christ, has complete control over the physical world—including the ability to help other people to conquer death.

Next we will ask if he possesses the power to do that very thing for himself.

PART FOUR

DESTINY

*   *   ✳   *   *

He faces his darkest hour. His time ends—and begins. A destiny is fulfilled.

From a common man—to all outward appearances—has emerged the universal Savior to bring light to the darkened world. A miracle worker, he has healed both body and soul—even raising the dead to life.

He has used his unique powers to fight the good fight. He has waged a never-ending battle for truth and justice. He has sacrificed his life in order to bring a better way to the oppressed and afflicted in all of humanity.

Tragically, those that need him most as a friend mistake him for an enemy. Yet he enables their salvation despite this. In a supreme act of sacrificial suffering, he dies. But this is not his end. Defeating even death, he comes alive again, eventually ascending into heaven.

Now the world waits for his return.

11

DEATH

* * ✳ * *

"Surely this man was the Son of God!"

THE ROMAN SOLDIER IN MARK 15:39

"In the ultimate sign of Christ-identification, Christ-figures frequently 'die' and then miraculously come back to life again," observes Anton Kozlovic of movies, including *Superman: The Movie*. Of course, the Superman story as a parallel to the gospel story would not be complete without the central events of the Christian faith: the death, burial, and resurrection of Christ. In fact, they are so important to the Superman story that they have been retold in symbolic and literal terms no less than four times within the Superman canon so far—not counting their inclusion in *Superman Returns*, which we will look at in chapter 14.

At the Hands of Lex Luthor

Often, within the death-burial-resurrection storyline, the figure most likely to drive the hero to his messianic destiny is the villain himself, which in turn emphasizes his own likeness to Lucifer. Here, his purpose, like the other biblical mirror figures, is to "set the scene and glorify the Christ-figure, no matter how indirectly." Appropriately, the first killer of the Superman Christ figure is one of his earliest enemies and the most famous of his foes.

> ### The Face of Luthor
>
> In 1940's *Action Comics* #23, when we first meet Lex Luthor, he has a full head of red hair—a shock of hair that is a shock to hindsight. By 1941, however, he is bald—as we know him today. In another change, while Lex was a mad scientist for 40 years straight, around the 1980s he gives into the zeitgeist and becomes a business tycoon, thereby revealing the modern face of pure evil—corporate America.

Displaying his most Lucifer-like trait, Lex Luthor hates Superman because of his power. Lex is intensely jealous because the Man of Steel possesses that which he desperately craves: the power of physical strength and, subconsciously, spiritual character. This is the reason Lucifer fell from angel to demon:

You said in your heart, "I will ascend to heaven; I will raise my throne above the stars of God; I will sit enthroned on the mount of assembly, on the utmost heights of the sacred mountain. I will ascend above the tops of the clouds; I will make myself like the Most High." But you are brought down to the grave, to the depths of the pit.[1]

To cement his association with the demonic, in the 1995 comic-book miniseries *Underworld Unleashed,* Lex makes a deal with the devil Neron—in exchange for the restoration of his deteriorating body, Luthor sells his soul. In this, Luthor is the ideal of the Nietzschean "superman," the man without need of his soul because he is his own God, recasting this struggle as Superman versus superman.

The Plot

In *Superman: The Movie,* Superman learns Lex Luthor (Gene Hackman) lives underground (a suitable location for the lair of a Lucifer figure.) When Lex presents to Superman his grand, twisted real-estate swindle—to blow up the San Andreas Fault and sink California into the sea, making the desert property he has bought very valuable—Luthor betrays another Lucifer-like characteristic, the devotion to the worldly kingdom. Lex makes an "indirect offer" to Superman which is refused, just as it is when Lucifer makes the offer to Christ:

> The devil took him to a very high mountain and showed him all the kingdoms of the world and their splendor. "All this I will give you," he said, "if you will bow down and worship me." Jesus said to him, "Away from me, Satan! For it is written: 'Worship the Lord your God, and serve him only.'"[2]

The movie's version makes the same point, albeit more bluntly.

> *Luthor:* Well, Superman? What do you think? Interesting?
> *Superman:* Your theory is quite impressive, Luthor. But as for the rest—it's nothing but a sick fantasy.

Hearing the refusal, Luthor reveals there are actually two missiles: one for California, one for New Jersey. He tricks Superman into looking for the detonation device in a lead trunk. Inside the trunk, the hero finds a kryptonite rock on a chain. He staggers back, weakened even at a distance. Lex wraps the chain around his neck, leads him to a ledge, and shoves him over. Superman drops into the pool below. Lex leaves him to drown slowly in a watery grave.

The Rising

Paul the apostle teaches that baptism by water—our lowering, immersion, and subsequent rising—is a symbol of Christ's death, burial, and subsequent resurrection. "We were…buried with him through baptism into death in order that, just as Christ was

Image: © Ohlinger Jerry/Corbis Sygma

Christopher Reeve as the icon incarnate in *Superman: The Movie.*
We have a friend in Jesus—and Superman. Reeve: "When Lois Lane asks, 'Who are you?' Superman simply responds, 'A friend.' I felt that was the key to the part: I tried to downplay being a hero and emphasize being a friend."

raised from the dead through the glory of the Father, we too may live a new life."[3] True to that progression, Superman sinks (death), remains under (burial), and then rises (resurrection) with the help of Lex's mistress, Miss Teschmacher (Valerie Perrine). Here, Teschmacher can be seen as a pre-redemption Magdalene who visits the crypt of the Savior, and even rolls away the stone.[4] Teschmacher removes the kryptonite rock, only after making Superman promise to stop first the missile headed toward New Jersey, where her mother lives. In a symbolic rebirth, the hero emerges from the water, resurrected from the pool in a scene suggestive of Jesus resurrected from the tomb.

Inviting further comparisons to the death of Christ, certain miraculous signifiers recur after the symbolic death of Superman:

* In the Bible, caused by the wrath of God, an earthquake shakes the land. In the movie, caused by the nuclear missile strike, an earthquake shakes the land.

* In the Bible, to save those lost long ago, Christ descends into Hades. In the movie, to save those on the land above, Superman descends into magma.

* In the Bible, at this time, the dead are raised to life. In the movie, as recounted before, Lois dies and is raised to life.

* In the Bible, Lucifer is disarmed and defeated to some extent. In the movie, Luthor is disarmed and defeated to a certain extent.

* In the Bible, with his work done for now, Christ ascends into heaven. In the movie, with his work done for now, Superman ascends into the heavens. (Notably, an ascension shot appears at the end of each Superman movie with Christopher Reeve.)[5]

At His Own Hand

A second symbolic death, burial, and resurrection storyline occurs in *Superman II*. This time there are three Kryptonian villains clad in black, the iconic biblical color of evil[6]: General Zod (Terence Stamp), Non the destroyer (Jack O'Halloran), and the woman Ursa, vicious and cruel (Sarah Douglas).

Devilish Enemies

While Zod was first seen in the April 1961 *Adventure Comics* #283, the characters of Non and Ursa were created for the movies. In the films, compared to Luthor, these three bear an even stronger resemblance to Lucifer (as well as mirroring three key figures from the book of Revelation). This is the evil trio found guilty of rebellion at the first of *Superman: The Movie*. To reestablish the scene, the court is in Krypton, our symbolic heaven. Their judge is Jor-El, our God figure. The Council of Elders numbers 12, like the apostles of Christ.[7] Given those elements, it follows these three criminals are cast in the role of the criminal archangel Lucifer.

Indeed, we find that the Lucifer-led war in the book of Revelation prefigures the Zod-led war in both personality and motivation. In the Bible, describing Lucifer as a dragon, John records,

> There was war in heaven. Michael and his angels fought against the dragon, and the dragon and his angels fought back. But he was not strong enough, and they lost their place in heaven. The great dragon was hurled down—that ancient serpent called the devil, or Satan, who leads the whole world astray. He was hurled to the earth, and his angels with him.[8]

Likewise, in *Superman: The Movie*, Jor-El describes in Luciferian terms

> this mindless aberration [Non] whose only means of expression are wanton violence and destruction...

Or the woman, Ursa, whose perversions and unreasoning hatred of all mankind have threatened even the children of the planet Krypton... And finally, General Zod. Once trusted by this Council, charged with maintaining the defense of the planet Krypton itself, the chief architect of this intended revolution and author of this insidious plot to establish a new order amongst us—with himself as absolute ruler.

Before being sentenced, Zod, a true Lucifer, tempts Jor-El with an offer of worldly power: "Yours could become an important voice in the New Order—second only to my own. I offer you a chance for greatness, Jor-El! Take it! Join us!" When temptation fails, Zod resorts to threats—which he even extends against Jor-El's family. "You will bow down before me! Both you, and then one day, your heirs!" In this, Zod echoes the dragon who threatens God's heir: "The dragon stood in front of the woman who was about to give birth, so that he might devour her child the moment it was born. She gave birth to a son, a male child, who will rule all the nations with an iron scepter. And her child was snatched up to God and to his throne."[9]

The three criminals are cast into the Phantom Zone (introduced along with Zod in the 1961 *Adventure Comics* #283, "The Phantom Superboy!"), a featureless dimension discovered by Jor-El from which detainees can observe, but cannot interact with, our dimension. Here, the Phantom Zone is a comic book equivalent to the biblical hell, or separately, the Abyss:

> I saw an angel coming down out of heaven...He seized the dragon, that ancient serpent, who is the devil....He threw him into the Abyss, and locked and sealed it over him, to keep him from deceiving the nations anymore until the thousand years were ended. After that, he must be set free for a short time.[10]

Death in Symbol

At the first of the 1981 *Superman II*, after we view a recap of the above events, we watch our hero save Paris by hurling a hydrogen bomb into outer space. By horrific happenstance, the bomb detonates near the Phantom Zone. The shockwaves crack the barrier and free the evil trio—coinciding with the just-cited scripture, the dragon "must be set free for a short time."

Meanwhile on Earth, with super-bad timing, Superman decides to surrender his powers to live a normal life with Lois—the Christ figure sacrificing himself for the love of another. In the script, and to a lesser extent in the movie, the scene seems like an alternate version of the time Christ spent in the Garden of Gethsemane[11]—a version in which the cup *could* be taken away, which underscores what Jesus gave up to meet death at the cross.

> *Jor-El:* Is this how you repay their gratitude? By abandoning the weak, the defenseless, the needy—for the sake of your selfish pursuits?
> *Superman:* Selfish! After all I've done for them? Will there ever come a time I've served enough? At least they get a chance for happiness! I only ask as much—no more.
> *Jor-El:* Yours is a higher happiness! The fulfillment of your missions! Your inspiration! You must have felt that happiness within you…My son, surely you cannot deny that feeling.*

When Superman asks if there is no other way, Jor-El reluctantly reveals a molecule chamber containing the red rays of the Kryptonian sun, which will remove Superman's powers.

Here, while the death scene is even more symbolic than in the first movie—it is exclusively Superman who dies while Clark

---

* These lines were scripted and shot for *Superman II,* but they do not appear in the original version of the film, where mother Lara replaces Jor-El. Some of this material may be seen on Richard Donner's new edit of *Superman II,* now available on DVD.

lives—the imagery involved is no less potent. Rising from below, the chamber that can extinguish his powers resembles a coffin. Once Superman enters the chamber, he sees visions that depict a descent into hell (Christ into Hades)—first he walks through fire, later his skin peels away, then his skeletal structure (a traditional death symbol) is laid bare. When the form of Clark finally steps out, he leaves behind a ghost image of Superman…which slowly fades into nothing.

A Savior Is Needed

In another part of the world, upon their arrival on Earth, the three supervillains assume three new roles—those of the Unholy Trinity of Revelation. Indeed, the plan of the evil trio on Earth seems lifted from the plan of the Unholy Trinity (see sidebar). Speaking of the beast, the agent of the dragon, the Bible states,

> He was given power to make war against the saints and to conquer them. And he was given authority over every tribe, people, language and nation. All inhabitants of the earth will worship the beast—all whose names have not been written in the book of life belonging to the Lamb that was slain from the creation of the world."[12]

> ## Zod, Non, and Ursa—The Unholy Trinity
> In the Bible, Lucifer, the Antichrist, and the False Prophet stand in opposition to God, Jesus Christ, and the Holy Spirit respectively. Figuratively, the movies pair up the same: Zod (Lucifer) to Jor-El (God), Non (Antichrist) to Superman (Christ), and Ursa (False Prophet) to Lois (seen here as the Holy Spirit). These three new identifications are accomplished through a series of biblical indicators seen in the sidebars on the next three pages.

Speaking on behalf of the evil trio, in the shooting script General Zod states,

> Today I bring a New Order to your planet! One which shall last until the end of time!...There is no longer a need for separate nations in this world... There is now one law, one order, one ruler who alone

will determine your collective destiny! One force before which all of you shall kneel forever!...From this day forward—there is only Zod!

Restoration

Elsewhere, at a roadside restaurant, hearing the news of the supervillains' invasion, Clark realizes his dreadful error. Desperate, he treks back through the arctic wasteland to the Fortress of Solitude. There, he hopelessly surveys the charred remains of the crystal control bank that overloaded when the chamber took his powers. In the script, to continue with the alternate version of the Garden of Gethsemane events, the scene shows how the unthinkable consequences of that deferred fate have been glimpsed to profound regret—emphasizing that for Clark, his destiny is his cross to bear. Clark speaks: "Father, if you can hear me, I have failed. I have failed you, myself, and all humanity. I have traded my birthright for a life of submission in a world now ruled by your enemies. There is no one left to help them, father, the people of the world. Not since I…" Clark stops, helpless and alone, then screams, "Father!" Suddenly, a faint green glimmer emerges and catches his eye. With hope, Clark gazes as a crystal glows green—the biblical color for new life[13]—the crystal that Jor-El placed in his spaceship, the one that led the teenage Clark to his calling, the one that built the Fortress of Solitude itself.

At this point, in the movie, the resurrection scene is implied rather than witnessed. However, in the script, Jor-El appears from the crystal—one last time.

Zod as Lucifer

As leader of the obscene three, Zod is again the Lucifer figure. He declares war on the offspring of his enemy as Lucifer declares war on the offspring of his enemy. "The dragon was enraged at the woman and went off to make war against the rest of her offspring–those who obey God's commandments and hold to the testimony of Jesus."[12] Zod is, after all, "evil incarnate," as the *Superman II* script describes him. "His only goal is to command a world of inferiors."

To underscore his divinity—evil as it is–in *Superman II*, when Zod first lands on Earth, he sinks into a pond, then raises himself and walks on water. One pivotal scene solidifies the similarities between Zod and Lucifer-who-would-be-God. After the evil trio takes over the White House, the president kneels and laments, "Oh, God." "Zod," the Kryptonian leader corrects.

(Again, the following lines were scripted and shot, but do not appear in the film.)

> *Jor-El:* Listen carefully, my son, for we shall never speak again…Once before, when you were small, I died while giving you a chance for life. And now, even though it will exhaust the final energy left within me—
> *Clark:* Father, no!
> *Jor-El:* Look at me, Kal-El! The Kryptonian prophecy will be at last fulfilled. The son becomes the father—the father becomes the son. Goodbye forever, Kal-El. Remember me, my son…

With that, Jor-El transfixes Clark with a bolt of energy, sacrificing himself to restore his son in a scene that transfers the messianic imagery to the father, who must reaffirm this ideal for his son. (The writer, Mankiewicz, had this example in mind: "It's God touching the hand of Adam as Jor-El touches his son and rejuvenates him.")

Triumph

As the movie continues, the resurrection is revealed in the next sequence as the restored Superman flies into Metropolis to fight the evil trio in an allegorical Armageddon. Finding the battle too dangerous for the citizens of the city, Superman flies off, leading the three villains, along with Luthor and Lois, back to the Fortress of Solitude for the final confrontation. Here, briefly, the image of one important Christ-associate

Non as the Antichrist

Non, the animal-like henchman of Zod, incarnates the Antichrist (or the beast), who is the animal-like henchman of the dragon Lucifer: "The beast I saw resembled a leopard, but had feet like those of a bear and a mouth like that of a lion. The dragon gave the beast his power and his throne and great authority."[14] Or as the *Superman II* script states, Non is a man "only to the extent that he is not an animal." Furthermore, the hulking henchman is "a force of frightening destruction" much like the beast of the dragon: "Men worshiped the dragon because he had given authority to the beast, and they also worshiped the beast and asked, 'Who is like the beast? Who can make war against him?'"[15] With the same question hanging in the air, in *Superman II,* a co-worker exclaims to Lois as they watch these two titans clash, "The big one is just as strong as Superman," thus confirming the pairing of Non the Antichrist figure to Superman the Christ figure.

Ursa as the False Prophet

Ursa, the beautiful but deadly killer, fulfills the figure of the False Prophet, who is the beautiful but deadly killer of the dragon and the beast. "I saw another beast, coming out of the earth. He had two horns like a lamb, but he spoke like a dragon."[16]

When Ursa enters a small-town diner, she gets hit on by a patron who is arm-wrestling. "Let's just hold hands," she purrs, and she offers a slender arm. When he grips her hand, she smashes his arm through the table.

Later, once she and Lois meet, they are the best of enemies. Ursa sizes up Lois: "What an undemanding male this Superman must be." Lois matches her: "You could use a tuck here and there yourself, sister." Both Lois and Ursa have apparent beauty, like the Holy Ghost and the False Prophet, but only Ursa the False Prophet figure uses her attractive appearance to hide an unholy spirit.

appears—one who has been conspicuously absent. Tired of Luthor again, Zod orders Non to kill him. Quickly, Luthor sides with Superman, extolling his honesty and integrity. Seemingly, Superman takes Luthor into his confidence, explaining that the chamber will take away the trio's powers. Immediately, Luthor informs Zod. In this, as the betrayer of our Christ figure, Luthor takes the place of Judas Iscariot. Lex sells out Superman as Judas sells out Jesus.[18]

Despite the betrayal by Luthor, upon being placed in the chamber, Superman de-powers the evil three by irradiating everything *but* the chamber in which he is protected with the red rays of the Kryptonian sun. Thereafter the three villains meet their fate by being cast into the icy, seemingly bottomless crevasses of the Fortress. The evil trio of the movie dies by ice; the unholy trinity of the Bible dies by fire:

> The devil, who deceived them, was thrown into the lake of burning sulfur, where the beast and the false prophet had been thrown. They will be tormented day and night for ever and ever.[19]

*   *   ✳   *   ·

Up till this point, the death and resurrection of Superman, our Christ figure, has been metaphoric, thus not truly reflecting the literal death and resurrection of Jesus Christ. However, true to the pattern of the Superman story in paralleling the gospel story, Superman is about to be subjected to the most challenging, painful, and frightening time of his life—to be ultimately followed by the most triumphant.

12

BURIAL

* * ✳ * *

He took it down, wrapped it in linen
cloth and placed it in a tomb.

Luke 23:53

The landmark "Death of Superman" comic-book storyline from 1992 to 1993 is distinguished from all other death, burial, and resurrection storylines within the Superman canon—and beyond. "They decided to kill Superman, and thus launched what proved to be the most widely discussed and publicized story in the history of the medium," says Les Daniels. In fact, the unprecedented interest generated by this storyline spurred efforts to bring Big Blue back to the big screen, and over a decade later these efforts have finally come to fruition in *Superman Returns*. Thus, while the 1992 storyline is entirely different from the one of 2006, if he had not died, he might not have returned.

Today, when people refer to the death of Superman, this is the storyline they mean. It is no surprise, then, that this story also proves to be the richest in biblical symbolism, mixing the imagery of the death, burial, and resurrection with the Bible's end-times prophecies and the second coming of Christ.

*   *   ✳   *   *

Our villain here, a behemoth known as Doomsday, again encompasses major biographical and personalistic elements of Lucifer. As we learn in the 1994 comic-book miniseries *Superman/ Doomsday: Hunter/Prey*, long ago on Krypton (heaven), the mad scientist Bertron (a corrupt God figure) planned to create a new life-form—an eternal one that cannot die. To do this, Bertron sends a normal life-form into the harsh wilderness, where it is quickly killed by the planet's deadly predators. Bertron then collects the remains, clones a new being, and sends it back into the wilderness—again and again and again—forcing it to adapt to survive. Finally, the creature is sent out and does not die but kills everything in its path, having grown to hate all life through innumerable deaths. When he returns to Bertron, Doomsday rebels against his father (like Lucifer does to his "father," God). Murdering the mad scientist, the evil creature departs from Krypton (like Lucifer cast out of heaven).

After years of causing death and destruction, Doomsday is finally defeated on another planet by an energy-being called the "Radiant"—a word in the Bible associated with God's presence.[1] Placed in a capsule, the lifeless body is launched up into space to eventually fall down to the Earth (like Lucifer), the alien coffin burying itself deep in the land.

The Superhero's Doom

In the *Death of Superman* collection, the pertinent issues of the first part of the story—his death—are contained under one cover. Here, the body of Doomsday, our latest Lucifer figure, is still bound and imprisoned inside the underground capsule, our newest representation of the abyss. However, while the body is still in the box, it is not still dead. Less a miracle than a damnation, after years of genetically enhanced adaptation, Doomsday has evolved past death. One massive fist has snapped its restraints, and it punches into the coffin wall over and over—until it breaks through.

As a resurrected beast that rises from an abyss, Doomsday matches the beast of the book of Revelation: "The beast, which you saw, once was, now is not, and will come up out of the Abyss and go to his destruction."[2] Once alive, then dead, now alive again, this Revelation beast, like Doomsday, symbolizes that evil will not truly die until the end of time when God destroys it.

Surfacing, Doomsday begins to carve a path of destruction that quickly endangers human lives; first he topples an interstate overpass, then he stops an 18-wheeler in a head-on collision with his free fist. Soon seven superheroes from the Justice League of America arrive. Probing the monster's mind for his identity, Maxima reports, "He's hate, death and blood lust personified"—which echoes the identity of "him who holds the power of death—that is, the devil."[3] Underestimating the power of Doomsday, the JLA gets taken apart.

Meanwhile, in an interview just before hearing about the monster, Superman is asked about his use of violence. In his reply, the Man of Steel forecasts the substitutionary suffering of his own death, while at the same time articulating the issue from a Christic perspective. "Believe me when I say I wish that violence wasn't necessary. But violence is the price we pay to accomplish a greater good. As heroes, we choose to protect that good with our lives."

Chasing the creature, Superman follows the actions of Doomsday, noting, "He just seems to wander from place to place, attacking whatever catches his eye." This resembles the actions of the devil, who "prowls around like a roaring lion looking for someone to devour."[4] To further link the two devils, Superman, who rarely curses, says Doomsday destroys "for the sheer hell of it!" Later, as a boy and a woman watch their hero in the fight of his life, the boy asks about Doomsday, and the woman answers, "I'd say he's the devil incarnate usherin' in the end of the world!"

In the confrontation, the Christic coloring continues. A particularly well-placed stab by Doomsday's spearlike elbow pierces Superman's right side—the same side in which Christ is pierced, according to tradition.[5] With blood flowing from the wound, Superman falls upside down with arms splayed out, his upper body in a crucifixion pose. Recovering, he tells Doomsday something Christ could tell the devil: "Your rampage ends here... even if it kills me." A line of narration with a messianic tone points to Superman: "Only one hope...one man remains."

Fatefully, Metropolis becomes the epicenter for the fight of the ages. Streets are demolished and cars are hurled as the indestructible fighters crash through buildings. A series of exploding gas and power lines, ruptured by the colossal combatants, shakes the city to its foundations. Ultimately, toe to toe, nose to nose, the two supreme opponents slug it out in front of the *Daily Planet*, mano a monster. Their final punches send shockwaves, shattering the glass from the windows. At the end, each puts his all into one last strike—which proves the killing blow for both.

The Darkest Day

In the moments after the death of Superman, the lines of narration that describe Jonathan and Martha Kent could describe Mary the mother of

---

Apocalypse

Doomsday is also known by another name: "The Armageddon Creature." In the book of Revelation, Armageddon is the place of the apocalyptic battle in which good meets evil and God defeats the forces of darkness. The cataclysmic imagery that informs the war in Metropolis is drawn from Armageddon: "They gathered the kings together to the place that in Hebrew is called Armageddon. The seventh angel poured out his bowl into the air, and out of the temple came a loud voice from the throne, saying, 'It is done!' Then there came flashes of lightning, rumblings, peals of thunder and a severe earthquake. No earthquake like it has ever occurred since man has been on earth, so tremendous was the quake. The great city split into three parts, and the cities of the nations collapsed."[6]

Jesus: For "those who would call him son, this is the darkest day they could ever imagine. They raised him to be a hero. To know the value of sacrifice. To know the value of life." Likewise, the lines that describe the members of the JLA could describe the apostles: "And for those who served with Superman in the protection of all life—comes the shock of failure. The weight of being too late to help." In order to save others, through the brutal bloodshed of the fight, Superman subjected himself to murderous punishment—assuming the image of the torturous surrender of Christ. The battle becomes analogous to the passion, in that each chronicles the sacrificial death of its world's Savior. The next step for both is burial.

In the *World Without a Superman* collection, where the part of this story—his burial—is contained, it is immediately made clear that Superman is in fact dead, rather than unconscious. (This is a common objection of skeptics to Christ's death and resurrection.) In the Superman story, the first proof of the Christ figure's death is brought by Dubbilex, a mind-reader: "I've been scanning Superman's mind, and there's nothing there—no brain-wave activity—nothing!"

Lois and Jimmy, in their roles as Magdalene and an apostle, are the first to attend to the body. The *Daily Planet* newspaper is again the gospel of Superman. Not only does Lois write about the passion of the fight, but Perry White, as John the Baptist, prophesies to Jimmy, "Olsen, one of these photos will serve to remind this city—no, the world, of the tremendous sacrifice one man made."

At the Kent home, watching the live reports on television, Ma and Pa have an overtly Christian response. Martha says, "What if they're right?" Jonathan replies, "We keep on praying to the good Lord for our boy, Ma." Later, a few news reporters offer eulogies for Superman that would also suffice for Christ: "The world will long remember this great man, who sacrificed his life to end the threat of Doomsday...God bless him." Another writes, "He inspired great passion in many people...but his greatest power was his compassion for his fellow man."

Among the inspired, Supergirl, a figurative and literal disciple of Superman, pledges to carry on his crusade for justice. Another, "Bibbo" (short for Bibbowski), owner of the Ace O'Clubs bar, prays, "God? I gotta ask ya...why? Why should Superman die...when a washed-up ol' roughneck like me goes on livin'?" This mimics a question familiar to many a Christian who recognizes the sacrifice Christ made and feels compelled to live a life that honors that act. (Later, Bibbo takes to the streets of his neighborhood to feed the hungry, help the poor, and even rescue puppies.)

Gone

The sky is dark in Metropolis the day Superman is laid to rest, recalling how "darkness came over the whole land" at the death of Christ, symbolizing God's sadness.[7] Ignoring the cold wind and rain, the faithful few from the *Daily Planet* and the JLA are joined by a crowd of thousands, who follow the funeral procession to the burial place in Centennial Park. Topped by a towering gold statue of the Man of Steel, the place the body is laid resembles a sacred shrine—although that is not what it is called. Notably, like the resting place of Christ, the resting place of Superman is referred to as a "tomb."

In Smallville, Ma and Pa Kent suffer a sharp insult added to injury, in that they cannot bury their son. Just as Mary

Doing What Is Right

Waverider, a time traveler, journeys back to the battle between Superman and Doomsday and freezes the killing blow to help the Man of Steel cheat death. In this temptation, Waverider is being tested by a senior time traveler named Matthew (like the biblical disciple and Gospel writer). In the image of his namesake, this Matthew says, "More has been written about this day than nearly any other."

Eventually, Waverider realizes, with Christic resonance, that to save Superman would be to raise him above others, which Superman himself would never do. And worse, it would discount the sacrifice Superman made with his life. He says to Superman: "You are nothing less than a miracle. But I am obligated to do the right thing." With that, he restarts time and watches Superman die.

To console Waverider, Matthew offers a message of hope, though somewhat cryptic: "The blessing...is, only we know what tomorrow will bring." So in the case of the death of Superman, as in the case of the death of Christ, knowing what tomorrow will bring is a blessing.

lost a son but the world lost a Savior, so Jonathan says, "We lost a son...but the world lost a hero...and they're gonna bury that hero with full honors." Instead, to bury Clark in their own way, the Kents take a few of his belongings to the field in which they first found their boy. Martha says of Clark what Mary must have thought of Jesus: "The sweetest little baby in the universe...our gift from heaven...and right from the start, we loved you with all our hearts. Heaven gave you to us...and now heaven has taken you." Tragically, Mary outlives her son, as Martha outlives hers.

Superman dies in the month of December—the month in which we celebrate the birth of Jesus. But as it is with Christ, Superman is dead only a few days when the tomb is found empty. When the motion detectors Lex Luthor has placed in the tomb are activated, Supergirl, ever the superdisciple, races over to investigate—and finds the coffin is not there. Later, in her reaction, Lois Lane seems to paraphrase Scripture: "Oh, Lord! It's empty! His tomb is empty!" Contrarily, one disbelieving Lex Luthor crony snorts, "Grave robbers. Some nut cases have stolen the body. That's the answer, pure and simple!" The biblical dismissal is similar: "You are to say," the Jewish leaders instruct the mystified tomb guards, "'His disciples came during the night and stole him away while we were asleep.'"[8]

In the Superman tale, the discovery is made on Christmas Eve. This seems ripe with promise for the rebirth of Superman on Christmas Day, in accordance with the birth of Jesus. And in a way, that promise is fulfilled. In a riff on the spurious story that the body of Christ was taken by his disciples, the body of Superman is taken by scientists. On Christmas Day, in a hidden lab, in a covert effort to raise Superman, genetic scientists begin to create a clone—the postmodern version of resurrection.

Outside the tomb, a group that worships Superman as a god (read, as *God*) sets up a vigil. The news reports that members "worship the late hero as a messiah and maintain that he will rise from the grave to carry on the never-ending battle." Each cult member wears a blue robe with the "S" shield on the front. Their leader speaks in pastoral language: "And I say to you, sisters and brothers, do not despair! In our hour of greatest need, Superman shall return to us from beyond the grave!" An acolyte raises her hands in praise, "Yes! He will return and save us all! Say the name! Say the name and be free!"

Later, Supergirl is able to retrieve the body from the scientists and return it to the resting place. Whereupon Lex, asking to be left alone in the tomb to pray, finally gets to deliver a particularly Luciferian speech over the closed coffin:

> So I win. I knew I'd bury you one day, you sanctimonious, self-righteous pain! I owned this town until you came along. There wasn't a man on earth who could stop me from doing whatever I pleased! And if anyone dared interfere—they were given a one-way ticket to hell.

A Father's Struggle with Death

Meanwhile, in Smallville, after reading the news that his son's body was stolen, Jonathan Kent suffers cardiac arrest.* In the hospital, Pa lies near death and encounters Clark in the afterlife. What he says to Clark he could say to Christ. "You've always saved everyone. Everyone but yourself. Why did you leave? Why did you have to die?" In a story entitled "Life after Death," with shades of the Christic descent into Hades, Pa pursues Clark when Kal-El is called into what appears to be a bright heavenly light. However, as a verbal hint to his actual location, Pa tells one antagonistic apparition, "You go straight to hell," then suspiciously asks himself, "Now what made me say that?"

At the foot of Pa's hospital bed, as Lois and Martha talk, religion enters the picture. Lois laments, "I guess if my faith were

---

* Interestingly, here Martha calls him "Jonathan *David*" Kent instead of "Jonathan *Joseph*," and even the name change carries Christic implications: The prophecies foretold that Christ would descend from David.[9]

stronger, I'd believe I could join Clark in an afterlife, Martha."
Martha replies, "Our faith believes in heaven, and Clark was
raised with those beliefs." Thus we learn conclusively that Clark
was raised as a Christian.

In hell, Pa continues his attempt to save Clark, recalling Christ
when he "preached to the spirits in prison."[10] Jonathan even confronts the devil Blaze, who tempts him with a deal: Clark's life
for Jonathan's soul. Pa refuses and soon finds a funeral procession
carrying Superman. Jonathan warns Clark, "You're on the wrong
path," which surely reminds us of Christ's message to the souls
in Hades. Heeding Pa, Superman realizes his Kryptonian spirit
guides are demons in disguise. Flying off with Jonathan, Superman
takes him to a shadowy tunnel in the sky—and hesitates. Pa, the
God figure again, says, "Have a little faith in your Old Man!"
Together, the two enter the tunnel. In the hospital room, Pa bolts
awake, claiming to have brought back Clark.

Is He Back?

A little later, arriving at the Metropolis airport, Lois listens to
news reports on eyewitness accounts of the return of Superman.
Shocked, she enlists the aid of a police friend to help her inspect
the tomb. Previously, at the tomb, the Superman worshippers have
grown in number—and symbolism. One has the "S" shield on
her forehead, like the mark of God on the foreheads of believers,
those who "had his name and his Father's name written on their
foreheads."[11] Another holds up a wooden cross with the "S" shield
where the perpendicular crossbeam would be. (Here, our earlier
idea that the "S" shield of Superman is a stand-in for the cross
of Christ is literally realized.) He shouts apocalyptically, "Be pre-
pared!" Yet another waves a sign reading, "He Died for You," and
cries out, "He'll come again!" One other sign features the word
"Savior" with the "S" shield in place of the letter "S."

Slipping past the worshippers, Lois and the inspector step
inside the tomb. There, not only do we find the place empty of
its occupant again—again so reminiscent of the former resting

place of Christ inspected by the apostles—but this time, the coffin remains, and the lid has been shoved off. As the inspector declares with a faith fervent enough to convert doubting Thomas, "I'd say from the look of things he's back! Superman's back!" His statement would prove more prophetic than present, as there were a few other scriptures this Superman story had to fulfill first.

13

RESURRECTION

* * ✳ * *

He is risen!

MARK 16:6

In the *Return of Superman* collection, leading up to the climactic event, even the individual story titles begin to reflect a more obvious use of religious overtones: "Born Again," "Alive," "An Eye for an Eye," "Lies and Revelations," "The Return," "Resurrections," and so on.

Four Apocalyptic Figures

At first, revealing the truth behind the reports of Superman's return, these stories relate the rise of four mysterious new supermen—which mirrors the rise of four mysterious biblical figures. In fact, to assign the biblical identifications of the four new supermen, a lady reading an article about them quotes the headline: "Are the New Supermen the Four Horsemen of the Apocalypse?"

In the Bible, the four horsemen of the Apocalypse—Conquest, War, Famine, and Death—represent God's judgment on the sin of mankind. In the Superman story, the four supermen share characteristics and signature colors with the four horsemen.

The Conqueror

John Henry Irons crawls up out of the rubble of the Superman/Doomsday battle believing the fight is still on, and he announces his good intentions: "Gotta stop Doomsday!" He is a muscular black man with a voice described as being like both "Darth Vader" and, more in line with our imagery, "the wrath of God." Days before the battle, Irons was at his construction job working the high steel on a skyscraper, when he fell and got saved by Superman. *Irons:* "I owe you my life!" *Superman:* "Then make it count for something!"

Irons does, by donning a high-tech metal suit fashioned after Superman's suit and becoming Steel. He is Conquest. "I looked and there before me was a white horse! Its rider held a bow, and he was given a crown, and he rode out as a conqueror bent on conquest."[1] A white knight in silver armor, with a noble spirit deserving of a crown, Steel substitutes the biblical bow for a massive hammer and rides out to conquer evil. Unlike the other three, he never claims to be Superman. "I wear this shield and this cape to honor a man who gave me back my life."

The Warrior

Superboy is a young clone of Superman, the clone made by the genetic scientists. He is otherwise known as Experiment 13—a number that biblically represents rebellion.[2] In fact, he is described as a rebel by the scientist from whom he escapes: "Oh, Thirteen gave me some trouble—started suddenly fighting off the input like a man possessed....We have absolutely no control over him!" With a chip on his shoulder the size of Superman, his first full sentence is, "Don't ever call me Superboy!" Arrogant, contentious, and impulsive—a dangerous mix for everyone around—he can also be sarcastically charming. Hit by a bus full of explosives, it's not the heat that makes him hot: "Okay—tryin' to kill me is one thing—but that was my only jacket! This means war!" And so he is War. "Then another horse came out, a fiery red one. Its rider was given power to take peace from the earth and to make men slay each other. To him was given a large sword."[3] Clad in red pants, red gloves, and red "S," the fiery color matches this do-gooder's disposition. It is Superboy who brings about the storyline's final war by leading the good men to the bad men.

Hunger

"The Last Son of Krypton" appears to be Superman in a new suit and a visor. He says to the first criminal he stops, in a style of judgment fit for the Old Testament, "I have passed through the fire and the darkness—and been changed! I have risen from the dead to continue the never-ending battle! I shall use the power that is mine as Krypton's last son to bring justice to this Earth. And all who sin shall know the vengeance of Superman!"

In fact, he is the Eradicator, a Kryptonian computer-being created to preserve Kryptonian life—at all costs—including, heartlessly, the suffering and even death of his enemies. His weakness is his famished hunger for energy, which he satisfies when he retrieves Superman's body—explaining its second disappearance—because the body converts solar energy into a form he can feed on (connoting Communion). He is Famine. "I looked, and there before me was a black horse! Its rider was holding a pair of scales in his hand...'A quart of wheat for a day's wages, and three quarts of barley for a day's wages.'"[4] He wears a suit with black sides and black arms; ultimately, his hunger causes him to drain dead the Fortress of Solitude as he powers up for a last-ditch effort to redeem himself and preserve the life of the true, risen Superman. This moral conversion for the Eradicator is described in biblical language:

> It had none of the passion, none of the love that
> Superman felt for our world. All emotions—whether

human or Kryptonian were alien to it. All that began to change when the Eradicator was reborn in the image of Superman. And may heaven help us all.

The Destroyer

Fourthly, the Cyborg superman is half man, half skeletal robotics. Though his features are baneful, at first he seems the most heroic of the new supermen: stopping a nuclear contamination leak, disposing of Doomsday's body in deep space, and saving the White House from a terrorist attack. His name is Hank Henshaw, a former astronaut bombarded by cosmic radiation that destroyed his body but enabled his consciousness to control circuitry and machinery.

With a burning hatred, he blames Superman for the loss of his humanity. Which is why, in the form of Superman, he causes the deaths of seven million men, women, and children by the decimation of a major metropolitan city in the largest explosion Earth has ever seen. He is Death—and Hades rides with him:

> I looked, and there before me was a pale horse! Its rider was named Death, and Hades was following close behind him. They were given power over a fourth of the earth to kill by sword, famine and plague, and by the wild beasts of the earth.[5]

With a pale metallic skull for a face, like the iconic skull face of death, he explains his plan, "I'll write Superman's legacy…and it'll be written in blood!" In assuming Superman's identity, eventually, he means to have the Man of Steel blamed for the destruction of the entire Earth.

The imagery surrounding the Cyborg also has strong associations to the Antichrist:

* In Revelation, the Antichrist is first described as "a beast coming out of the sea."[6] In the *Return of Superman*, the

Cyborg destroys Coast City, a city by the sea—from which the heretofore hero emerges as a beast.

*   In Revelation, "One of the heads of the beast seemed to have had a fatal wound, but the fatal wound had been healed. The whole world was astonished and followed the beast."[7] In the *Return of Superman,* the Cyborg's metallic skeletal face and exposed cranium indicate a fatal head wound. Yet because the villain insists he is the healed Superman, many are astonished and follow him, including the White House.

*   In the book of Revelation,

> The beast was given a mouth to utter proud words and blasphemies and to exercise his authority for forty-two months. He opened his mouth to blaspheme God, and to slander his name and his dwelling place and those who live in heaven.[8]

In the *Return of Superman,* the Cyborg blasphemes Superman by claiming to be him while planning to slander his name as the destroyer of the world. When the risen Superman and the Eradicator confront the Cyborg, the beast mocks the Man of Steel: "You drove me away because you feared I was more powerful than you! Now the universe will blame you for Earth's destruction!" Because the Eradicator also lived on Krypton (heaven), he is called a "piece of Kryptonian trash."

*   In Revelation, as we saw previously in regard to *Superman II,* the beast "was given power to make war against the saints and to conquer them. And he was given authority over every tribe, people, language and nation."[9] In the *Return of Superman,* boasting to his secret accomplice, the Cyborg proclaims his ultimate goal: "Earth will be damned!" Not only does he intend to wage war against Earth, but he will then remake Earth into a "warworld," a world dedicated to conquering other planets.

The Evil Accomplice

In the book of Revelation, the accomplice to the beast comes out of the earth and he "exercised all the authority of the first beast on his behalf, and made the earth and its inhabitants worship the first beast, whose fatal wound had been healed."[10] In the *Return of Superman*, Mongul, a former warlord dethroned by Superman, is the accomplice of the Cyborg. On behalf of the Cyborg, Mongul brings his warship to Coast City to dominate the area and its inhabitants.

In Revelation, this second beast "performed great and miraculous signs, even causing fire to come down from heaven to earth in full view of men."[11] In the *Return of Superman*, Mongul causes fire to come down from heaven to earth as he drops 77,000 bombs, which level the city in an explosion that stretches on past the three-minute mark.

In Revelation, the second beast "set up an image in honor of the beast who was wounded by the sword and yet lived. He was given power to give breath to the image of the first beast, so that it could speak and cause all who refused to worship the image to be killed."[12] In the *Return of Superman*, Mongul erects Engine City, a monstrous tribute to the Cyborg. In actuality a rocket engine the size of a city, Engine City will push Earth out of its orbit, turning it into a marauding warworld, which will kill all who refuse to bow down in worship. Talk about using the Bible as a blueprint!

Who Is the Savior?

Meanwhile, back at the tomb, furthering the end-times imagery, the Superman worshippers have split along denominational lines: Savior Cyborg and Savior Eradicator. One of the Savior Cyborgers sermonizes thus: "Look not upon our Savior's face with fear…though he bears the marks of his righteous battle against the terrible beast Doomsday…Be not deceived by the smooth, unblemished face of the visored impostor…I say unto you, he is a fraud." Then from the Savior Eradicator side: "Fools…You worship a graven image come to an unholy life!" Another: "Yeah, why don't you worship a golden calf an' make a clean job of it?" Here, a rare overt reference is made to the Hebrew God whom the Israelites anger by worshipping a golden calf,[13] which leaves no question as to whom these worshippers perceive their Superman to be—if there is a God of the Old Testament, then his dead, buried, and resurrected agent must be the Christ.

Speaking of which, all of the above naturally follows what the original Super Man said about the end times:

Jesus answered: "Watch out that no one deceives you. For many will come in my name, claiming, 'I am the Christ,' and will deceive many. You will hear of wars and rumors of wars, but see to it that you are not alarmed. Such things must happen, but the end is still to come. Nation will rise against nation, and kingdom against kingdom. There will be famines and earthquakes in various places. All these are the beginning of birth pains."[14]

Christ concludes, "False Christs and false prophets will appear and perform great signs and miracles to deceive even the elect."[15]

Rebirth

The climactic moment, the rebirth of Superman, is actually presented in three different images, all of them involving water—recalling what Paul tells us about the death, burial, and resurrection symbolized in baptism. First, when the Eradicator retrieves Superman's body, he places it in the "healing baths" of an egg-shaped energy pod. One day, suddenly, the egg overloads and explodes. Superman slowly stirs to life—though weak, without his full powers. To return to Metropolis, he climbs inside a two-story Kryptonian war suit, wherein he is suspended in a fetal position in a "nutrient-rich amniotic womb," as Scott Beatty calls it. Conspicuously, instead of flying, the suit travels under the water across the ocean floor. Finally, upon reaching Metropolis, he is expelled from the suit in explicit birthing imagery: the war suit opens a hatch between its legs, the liquid pours out, and Superman drops down onto the ground.

It is notable that no one takes his resurrection for granted. In fact, to emphasize what an extraordinary event this is, most of the major characters express doubts. In these doubts, they depict the two schools of thought among skeptics of Christ's death and resurrection. Superboy supposes that, if he is alive now, then he could not have been dead: "Then he never died?" The others suppose that, if he did die, then he cannot be alive now. *Lois:* "People—even Superman—can't come back from the dead!" *Steel:* "Maybe it is him. I want it to be him. But Superman died." *Cyborg:* "No!! He's dead!! Dead and gone!! Superman can't possibly be alive. Can he?"

However, as Christians would attest of Christ, so the conversation between Superman and the Eradicator leaves no doubt as to the literal death and resurrection Superman has experienced:

> *Superman:* But I wasn't dead! I was just in a kind of a coma or something! Right?
>
> *Eradicator:* Thoughts such as those may comfort you, but you must understand—you were categorically deceased, Kal-El...Only by getting to you quickly—and administering the healing baths of the matrix chamber—could I help...In fact, it's safe to say this would not be possible ever again.

Here, we must note that the Eradicator's explanation only pertains to the physical body. To account for the return of the soul, we must remember the work Jonathan Kent did when he descended into hell and saved his son's spirit.

For reasons cited above, the final fight between Superman (the risen Christ figure) and Cyborg (the Antichrist figure) resounds with resurrection–second coming–end times imagery, telescoping past, near future, and far future events. As Superboy says, "We're talking end of the world stuff here..." Ultimately though, in line with the biblical narrative, good defeats evil. Nevertheless, before this storyline is over, we must mention that, unfortunately, Superman is not the only one who rises from the dead. As mentioned earlier, shortly after the arrival of the four supermen, the Cyborg binds Doomsday's corpse to an asteroid and hurls it deep into space. Later, horrifically, it is revealed that Doomsday, our cautionary symbol of resurgent evil, has come back to life, awake and laughing in the infinite darkness. He is fearful of only one day, as is all evil, a day when the good will rejoice—and that is the day when one man is seen again, the day when the Super Man returns.

Another Resurrection

Briefly, showing the influence of the "Death of Superman"

as well as the passion of Christ, *Smallville* recently presented a surprisingly corporeal death and resurrection for Clark in an episode entitled "Hidden" (#91). Earlier, young Clark loses his powers when he fails to return to Jor-El at the Fortress of Solitude. Now, Clark is trying to stop another teenager from launching a nuclear missile to destroy Smallville and rid the town of the Kryptonite "mutants."

The adolescent villain's name is Gabriel. The biblical Gabriel is the angel who announces the birth of Christ.[16] This Gabriel will herald our Christ figure's death as he shoots Clark in the waist. Clark falls to the ground with arms spread out to each side and knee bent—the death position of the crucifixion. To complete the iconic image, the bullet has pierced his side, and blood flows freely from the wound—just as the side of Christ is pierced, causing blood and water to flow freely from the wound, confirming Jesus is dead.[17]

Later, at the hospital, Clark dies, his life sacrificed in the service of others. A sheet is pulled over his body, as the body of Jesus was wrapped "in a clean linen cloth." Moments later, the hospital room is found empty, the vacant sheet still on the bed—similar to the tomb in which "they did not find the body of the Lord Jesus," but only "the strips of linen lying by themselves."[18]

Clark comes back to life in the Fortress of Solitude, transported there by his father Jor-El. Their exchange confirms the physical death, resurrection, and return of power Clark has experienced. *Clark:* "Am I dead?" *Jor-El:* "Your mortal journey is over, yes. But your imminent destiny is too important to be sacrificed. You will return, with all of your natural gifts." He then tells Clark that soon someone will give their life for his, perhaps prophesying the figure of the first martyr for our savior in the series. (It appears later that the martyr is Jonathan Kent, in episode #100.)

After his rising, Clark races to stop the launched missile, jumping on board for a ride heavenward, capping off the sequence with striking Christic ascension imagery. As Lex later notes to Lana with growing suspicion of Clark, "I heard about Clark's resurrection. You know, I've never really believed in miracles, but I've certainly done my share of asking for them today." A minute passes, and he phrases his feelings more directly: "A normal person doesn't rise from the dead."

Just wait till he returns from the heavens.

14

Second Coming

* * ✳ * *

*"The Son of Man will come at an hour
when you do not expect him."*

JESUS, IN LUKE 12:40

* * ✳ * *

In this chapter we will discuss speculation about the plot of
Superman Returns *drawn from various sources, concentrating on
those points that bear on our topic. If you have not seen the film and
do not want the plot potentially spoiled, do not read the analytical
sections of the following chapter (starting on page 151) until after you
have seen* Superman Returns.

* * ✳ * *

A Devoted Follower

Director Bryan Singer (*X-Men, X-Men 2*), a tremendous fan of the Richard Donner–directed *Superman: The Movie*, recalls "that film, particularly its first act, was a complete day-to-day inspiration to the first X-Men film for all of us." So devoted is Singer to *Superman: The Movie* that years ago he sought Donner's blessing on the storyline for his new movie. Furthermore, because we know the Donner film portrays Superman as a Christ figure, it is intriguing to note Singer says he plans to "protect some semblance of this character" that Donner presents to us. In another example of his dedication to the first film, Singer will incorporate footage of Marlon Brando as Jor-El, the God figure, into *Superman Returns*. (The new movie may even carry this dedication: "In memory of Christopher Reeve.")

Anticipation is high for the second coming of Superman—as is illustrated by the royal treatment of the new movie in a typical article: "Here in the golden age of the superhero flick," *Entertainment Weekly* holds forth, "there has been no shortage of princes. Spider-Man. Batman. The X-Men. Yet all are mere pretenders to a long-vacant throne. On June 30, 2006, Warner Bros. gives us the return of the king—otherwise known as *Superman Returns*." Nearly 20 years after the last Superman movie, 10 years after efforts began to welcome him back, after one false sighting (*Superman Reborn* or *Superman Lives*—both titles inviting Christic comparisons), finally the Man of Tomorrow has come again.

A kind of "threequel" to *Superman: The Movie* and *Superman II*, the movie *Superman Returns* begins five years after the events seen in the earlier films. Director Bryan Singer describes its storyline this way:

It's not an origin story; I didn't want to remake what Richard Donner did so well in the original, and didn't want to tread on the great work they're doing on *Smallville*. He's already part of the culture; he has left the planet. This is the story of his return.

A little later, Singer puts a finer point on his vision of the return, again revealing a fondness for making connections between Superman and Jesus: "It's a story about what happens when messiahs come back and how we embrace them—or not."

Ultimately, in the great tradition of *Superman: The Movie*,

Singer makes the Christic symbolism explicit for *Superman Returns:**

> Superman is the Jesus Christ of superheroes. So it's sort of the American dream combined with a little bit of the myth, the concept of Messiah. There's a lot of that in the movie. It's not huge, not religious. But there's very much a hint of that. It's like X-Men deals with a lot of tolerance, in a very sub-textual way. I think that Superman deals a lot with saviors and things like that.

And one of the writers for the movie has publicly concurred. When asked what other comic hero he might like to write, screenwriter Dan Harris just smiles: "There's nowhere to go from [Superman]. This is the Jesus Christ of superheroes. Like, where do you go?"

Anticipation and Speculation

The official plot synopsis is sketchy:

> Following a mysterious absence of several years, the Man of Steel comes back to Earth in the epic action-adventure *Superman Returns,* a soaring new chapter in the saga of one of the world's most beloved superheroes. While an old enemy plots to render him powerless once and for all, Superman faces the heartbreaking realization that the woman he loves, Lois Lane, has moved on with her life. Or has she? Superman's bittersweet return challenges him to bridge the distance between them while finding a place in a society that has learned to survive without him. In an attempt to protect the world he loves from cataclysmic destruction, Superman embarks on an epic journey of redemption that takes him from the depths of the ocean to the far reaches of outer space.

---

* In an interview with *Wizard: The Comics Magazine.*

To delve deeper into this "epic journey of redemption," here we will take a look at some of the plot speculation. (Though our discussion may not reflect the actual plot points of the film, again, if you do not want the plot *potentially* spoiled, see *Superman Returns* before reading further.)

Second Advent

When the story begins, Superman (our Christ figure) has ascended into the heavens (like Christ) to return to Krypton (heaven). He has gone there to confirm that he is in fact the Last Son. Finding a "graveyard" where his home planet used to be, Superman (played by Brandon Routh) returns to Earth, arriving again around five years after he first left. This period of time is symbolic of the time between Christ's ascension and his return—a time during which, in both the biblical narrative and the Superman story, conditions on Earth deteriorate during the absence of the Savior.

In his starship—a larger version of the little star-of-Bethlehem ship from *Superman: The Movie*—Superman again crash-lands in a Kansas cornfield near the Kent farm. The fiery, earthshaking imagery reflects not only the literal second coming of Superman but a figurative version of the literal second coming of Christ. Similarly, when Christ returns "'the stars will fall from the sky, and the heavenly bodies will be shaken.' At that time men will see the Son of Man coming in clouds with great power and glory."[1]

Love Grown Cold

Clark recuperates at the Kent farm before returning to Metropolis—to something less than a hero's welcome. In the time he was away, people have come to resent Superman. Once he left, the world fell into chaos, and their dependence on him became painfully obvious. Because of their pride, what they really disdain is their own weakness, their undeniable need for a Savior, as is often the case with people who resent Christ. In their desperation, the people of Metropolis have grown cold, as have those waiting

Brandon Routh, playing the Man of Tomorrow as the Second-Coming Man in *Superman Returns*. Routh on what troubles the soul of Superman, with a Christic echo: "If I was here before and that's all they think that I'm here for, to save things, maybe there's more to my destiny…that's imparting some kind of wisdom to the world in some other way."

for the return of the true Messiah during times of tribulation: "Because of the increase of wickedness, the love of most will grow cold, but he who stands firm to the end will be saved."[2]

Even Lois Lane (Kate Bosworth) exhibits this loss of faith. She writes an article for the *Daily Planet* that includes the almost anti-Christic line: "The world doesn't need a savior. And neither do I." This is the biggest surprise for Superman and also the most heartbreaking: Lois, the love of his life, with whom he was romantically involved in *Superman II,* has left him behind. She and a man named Richard White (James Marsden) are engaged to be married and are raising a child.

The Enemy Rampant

Meanwhile, Lex Luthor (Kevin Spacey) has been released from the abyss of prison like Lucifer is released from the prison of the abyss. (When Superman left to return to Krypton, so also went the key witness against the criminal mastermind.) Freed, Lex raids the Fortress of Solitude and steals any artifact of Kryptonian technology he can find. It is assumed that among the items is the green crystal which built the Fortress. Luthor realizes the land-forming capabilities of the crystal and decides to use it to create real estate—like Lucifer, still displaying an unhealthy obsession with a worldly kingdom. When Luthor raises a landmass in the middle of the ocean, the consequences are apocalyptic—earth-quakes, tidal waves, and flooding threaten to tear the planet apart, evoking the damage caused at Armageddon: "Every island fled away and the mountains could not be found."[3]

When Superman arrives to stop him, Luthor stabs him with a kryptonite dagger. Rushed to the hospital, he lies near death from the wound, his deathbed assuming the symbolism of the cross. Outside, in the rain (sign of God's sadness), the citizens of Metropolis rally behind their fallen superhero. Some hold signs: "Save Our Superman," "I Love Superman" and "Superman, Don't Die!" A prayer vigil is set up.

Back inside the hospital, not only has Superman lost too

much blood, but what blood he has left has been poisoned by the kryptonite dagger. It is critical for him to receive a blood transfusion immediately, however, there is no one on Earth who has his blood type. Or is there?

Revival

At this point, it seems likely, Lois enters the room with her child. Her son is around five years old, the same number of years Superman has been away. His first name is *Jason*, which means "healer" or "God is my Savior." It is rumored his middle name is *Christopher*—"Christ-bearer." If this is so, his first two initials are J.C. His last name is *White*, again, the signature color of the divine.

Though White is the last name of her fiancé, Lois reveals that Richard White is not Jason's father. The boy is Superman's son, the result of their romance in *Superman II* (a boon to those fans of Jesus-and-Magdalene romantic apocrypha!). With the shifting of the Savior role over to the boy, Superman is saved from death through the transfusion process and resurrected by the blood of the son. (Indeed, the name *Jason* comes from the name *Joshua*—actually the same name as *Jesus*—which, of course, means "God saves.")

Upon his revival, Superman confronts Luthor again. Defeating the evil villain once and for all (once again), he presumably banishes Luthor to a prison as Lucifer is banished to the lake of fire. Thereafter, Superman lifts the landmass Luthor created with the Kryptonian crystal. He hurls "New Krypton" from the sea into the heavens, where it takes its place among the stars, reminiscent of the new heaven and new earth that will be the home of God and his followers: "I saw a new heaven and a new earth,

References and Resonances

The working title of *Superman Returns* is *Red Sun*, which is the name of the production company as well. While the title is a reference to the red sun of Krypton, "red sun" also carries covert Christic resonances. As we've seen, red stands biblically for blood. *Sun* is a phonetic match to *son*. Put together then, the two-name title offers wordplay on the secret subject of the story: "Red Sun" translates to "Blood Son."

for the first heaven and the first earth had passed away, and there was no longer any sea."[4] And, as in the biblical narrative, everyone in the Superman story lives happily eternally after.

*   *   ✱   *   *

One image from the new film has already made an indelible impression. At the end of the teaser trailer, Superman floats above the Earth in the silence of space. He is listening with his eyes closed, as if to prayers, trying to hear where he is needed. The voice of Jor-El (the late Marlon Brando) is heard to say the legendary lines that forever confirmed Superman as a Christ figure: *They can be a great people, Kal-El—they wish to be. They only lack the light to show the way. For this reason above all, their capacity for good, I have sent them you—my only son.* Superman hears a cry, and he lunges downward, rocketing toward earth, a sonic boom in his wake. That's our Savior figure; that's the image of our Lord Jesus Christ.

Jesus Christ, Superhero

* * ✳ * *

Superman reflects Christ. Each chapter in this book has pointed out some aspect of this. There's another question, a very reasonable one, to be asked, though: Doesn't the figure of Superman reflect other divine figures? My answer is, in a word, no. The attraction of Superman to humankind is actually the attraction of no one else but Christ.

At this statement, media-age atheists will protest that the appeal of the Superman story has never been salvation, but *escapism*. With good justification, they point to aspects of comic-book fantasy (rather than godly truth) and science fiction (rather than Christic fact). Nonetheless, to the extent we respond favorably to a Christ figure like Superman, we do not *escape* from reality—we are instead drawn closer to the reality of Christ. Look at his words. He tells us there is a time for rest: "Come to me, all you who are weary and burdened, and I will give you rest." Yet he also tells us there is never a time for being away from him: "Surely I am with you always, to the very end of the age."[1] So even in our rest, we rest in him; even in our escapism, we escape to him.

And in our great search for purpose in our existence, we find our purpose in him.

A Modern Myth?

For their part, agnostics will contend that the entire Superman story is just a modern reflection of the world's religious myths. For instance Slayter Brown writes that Superman "embodies all the traditional attributes of the Hero God...He is, moreover, a protective deity....The comic strip seems to fill some symptomatic desire for a primitive religion." It's indeed true that some of the earliest religious myths, as Christian theologian R.C. Sproul Jr. concedes, "have as a part of their story, not only a flood myth, but even a dying and rising God." Since many religious stories feature Christ figures that pre-date Christ, critics of Christianity have argued that the existence of these older narratives indicates the Christ story is a borrowed, man-made myth.

To counter this, Sproul paraphrases C.S. Lewis, who

> argued not only that these myths were not evidence against the Christian faith, but that they were evidence for it. He reasoned that these myths demonstrated that the message of the cross was built into the very nature of reality.

The cross is "built into reality" because our reality is built on it—as the book of Revelation tells us, Christ is "the Lamb that was slain from the creation of the world."[2] In the eternal counsels of God, the story of the cross was told before the story of our world began. Scholar Jill Carattini concurs. While there are elements in myth that we want to believe, "Christianity would take this one step further," she notes. "It would argue that these are actually the stories that we knew on some real level had to be true. In myth, mankind has revealed what is engraved deeply on our hearts."

Concerning the Christ myth, Lewis himself explains,

> It is God's myth where the others are men's myth:

> i.e., the Pagan stories are God expressing Himself
> through the minds of poets, using such images as
> He found there, while Christianity is God expressing
> Himself through what we call "real things."

Later, Lewis summarizes this thought: "We must not be nervous about 'parallels' and 'pagan Christs': they ought to be there—it would be a stumbling block if they weren't."

As much as they may disagree with this reasoning, challengers should realize Lewis is making quite a generous concession. Why? Because there are in fact no literal pre-Christ figures. Though we can use this term for figures found in earlier savior stories that have superficial similarities to Jesus, under closer scrutiny, these similarities do not support an actual match to Jesus—certainly nowhere near the match of Superman to Christ. If we make a comparison of these two Saviors to well-known deities of other world religions—well, there is no real comparison.

Possible Substitutes?

Critics will commonly try to identify Jesus with other deities through the events of his death and resurrection. They attempt to place Christ—or even Superman—in the same league with a handful of usual suspects: the "dying and rising gods" (for example, Adonis, Baal, Osiris), the gods of the mystery religions (for example, Dionysos, Isis), and world religion figures (Buddha, Krishna, and so on).

In all these attempts, critics quickly run into problems. From the dying and rising gods gallery, *Adonis* moves from the underworld to the land of the living *before* he dies; after he dies, while his death is recreated annually, he is never actually resurrected. *Baal,* supposedly a prime example of a dying and rising

The Golden Bough Is Broken

The concept of dying and rising gods, originally championed by James Frazer, author of *The Golden Bough,* has since been refuted. Walter Burkert writes, "The Frazerian construct of a general 'Oriental' vegetation god who periodically dies and rises from the dead has been discredited by more recent scholarship....There is a dimension of death in all of the mystery initiations, but the concept of rebirth or resurrection of either gods or *mystai* is anything but explicit."

Nothing to Believe In?

It is not at all clear how much the pagans believed in their own gods. G.K. Chesterton would ask, Where are the pagan martyrs, willing to sacrifice all to defend their faith? Likely they were too busy winking at the idea of a mythic deity.

Indeed, the Greeks had a specific date to mark the turning point between fictional myth and factual history. This date was set by the historian Ephorus (about 405 to 330 BC) as the time of "the return of Hercules' offspring to the Peloponnesus [peninsula], where their ancestor had once held sway. Traditionally this was the way of referring to the arrival of the Dorians in the peninsula, c. 1070 BC," according to Peter G. Bietenholz.

By contrast, the living Jesus is recorded in the history books of both Josephus, a Jew, and Tacitus, a Roman.

god, not only does not die, but does not rise. He descends to the underworld and returns only "as if" he is dead. *Osiris,* after his murder, does not return to life; on the contrary, he becomes the king of the dead.

Nor do the mystery religions fare any better. *Dionysos,* although called a twice-born god, was actually taken from his mother's womb, sewn into Zeus's thigh, and emerged three months later in his first and only birth. And the initiate into *Isis* is promised neither resurrection nor eternal life with her, but only that when he dies, he may continue to worship her in the land of the dead.

In fact, as MacMillan's *Encyclopedia of Religion* comments, all the gods "that have been identified as belonging to the class of dying and rising deities can be subsumed under the two larger classes of disappearing deities or dying deities. In the first case, the deities return but have not died; in the second case, the gods die but do not return. There is no unambiguous instance in the history of religions of a dying and rising deity"—apart from Jesus Christ.

Of the world religion figures, like some of the gods above, both *Buddha* and *Krishna* die, and neither come back to life. More importantly here, during their lives, they reveal fundamental differences from Christ. While young Krishna steals, lies, and lusts, young Jesus discusses Scripture in the temple. Whereas the enlightened Buddha says there is no savior, the Son of God gives his life to save others. Meanwhile, Superman fights for truth and justice—in stark contrast to Buddha and Krishna.

The One and Only

Confirming the above, three major distinctions set Christ's death apart from all others.

1. Christ dies in the place of someone else. This substitution is a notion unique to Christianity.

2. Christ dies purposefully to help other men. None of the so-called savior gods die with this intention.

3. Christ dies of his own free will. Possibly Hercules and, in some stories, Attis kill themselves—that's the best they've got. Superman, on the other hand, also dies substitutionally, purposefully, and voluntarily, following the pattern of Christ.

A careful comparison of these deities' dying and rising to the literal death and resurrection of Christ demonstrates that, as we said previously, there really is no comparison at all. So, when Superman literally dies and literally rises again, he does so not in the likeness of these gods—for that likeness never existed—but rather in the image of the one true Savior who conquered death to live anew.

Where the Story Takes Us

Christian writers C.S. Lewis and J.R.R. Tolkien consciously chose to present "deep myths" to the general public in much of their fiction, as Craig Johnson notes: "They did this knowing that by so plucking their reader's spiritual and emotional heart strings, they could, thereby, better prepare the way for a later acceptance of the Gospel of Jesus Christ."

Gary Engle puts his finger on the "deep myths" in the Superman story in these words:

> ### Rediscovering the Awe
> Louis Markos suggests a positive use of pagan myths in fostering Christian conversion: "If we are to win back the neopagans, we need to rediscover our awe at the majesty of God and his Creation, an awe that has little to do with the current warfare over worship styles and everything to do with that breathless sense of the numinous that we first encountered in…a timeless tale from mythology or folklore or legend…."

> Superman is like nothing so much as an American
> boy's fantasy of a messiah...[He has come] from
> heaven to deliver humankind by sacrificing himself
> in the service of others. He protects the weak and
> defends truth and justice and all the other moral
> virtues inherent in the Judeo-Christian tradition,
> remaining ever vigilant and ever chaste.

More pointedly, as evildoer after evildoer is caught and convicted, Superman "demonstrates a remarkable capacity for effecting personal salvation," as Michael Mautner puts it. While this salvation certainly comes to those *in* the story, as we've seen throughout, it can also be true for those *outside* the story—the readers. As Scott Beatty points out, the appeal of the Man of Steel, as always, draws us upward to something—or Someone—greater:

> With the timeless character of Superman, Siegel
> and Shuster didn't just create the world's most
> beloved comic book hero. They created the ideal
> hero, whose unflagging virtue and undefeatable
> optimism inspire every single one of us to want to
> be just like him.

Amen.

*   *   ✳   *   *

Thus, we end where we began. Yet I hope we're not the same, because each encounter with a Christ figure should bring us closer to Christ. Believers can discover a new way to reach those who are seeking. Seekers can discover something closer to the truth. Together, they can find common ground.

If *The Gospel According to the World's Greatest Superhero* is in fact a dim shadow and a bright reflection of the Gospel of Jesus Christ, we should expect nothing less.

That is the story I recall encountering so vividly back at

Christmastime 1978. Perhaps that means, after all this time, I still have childlike faith. I consider that a great thing. It is a selfish and cynical world we live in, and the spirit of Luthor always threatens to extinguish the light. I, for one, will hold fast to that memory of being six years old at Christmastime, sitting in the darkened theater next to my father, when I was touched with wonder, held in awe by the image of a story larger than myself, grander than all the rest of us—a story I longed to be a part of, that I finally am part of. And during dark days, when I think back on that time, I realize it's still true. Thank God, it's still true. I still believe a man can fly.

*   *   ✳   *   *

RECOMMENDED READING AND VIEWING

* * ✳ * *

LIST OF SOURCES

Beatty, Scott. *Superman: The Ultimate Guide to the Man of Steel.* New York: DK Publishing, 2002.

Bruce, David. "Superman, 1978," www.hollywoodjesus.com, October 1998.

Carattini, Jill. "Myth became History," *A Slice of Infinity* (Ravi Zacharias Ministries), July 21, 2003. Article can be viewed online at www.gospelcom.net/rzim/publications/slicetran.php?sliceid=423.

Daniels, Les. *Superman: The Complete History.* San Francisco: Chronicle Books, 1998.

Engle, Gary. *Superman at Fifty! The Persistence of a Legend!* New York: Collier Books, 1988.

Friedrich, Otto. "Up, Up, and Awaaay!!!," *Time* magazine, cover story (March 14, 1988).

Gough, Alfred. *Smallville—The Complete First Season* DVD. Burbank, CA: Warner Home Video, 2003, ep. 1.

Hooper, Walter, ed. *The Letters of C.S. Lewis to Arthur Greeves (1914-1963).* New York: Macmillan Publishing Company, 1979.

———. *Of Other Worlds: Essays and Stories.* London: Geoffrey Bles, 1966.

Johnson, Craig. "That for Which You Dream Is True..." Bethel Christian Fellowship Web site. Article can be viewed online at www.drcraigjohnson.org/rings.html.

Kozlovic, Anton Karl. "The Holy, Non-Christic Biblical Subtexts in *Superman: The Movie* (1978) and *Superman II* (1981)," *Journal of Religion and Film,* vol. 6, no. 2 (October 2002).

———. "Superman as Christ-Figure: The American Pop Culture Movie Messiah," *Journal of Religion and Film,* vol. 6, no. 1 (April 2002).

———. "The Unholy Biblical Subtexts and Other Religious Elements Built into *Superman: The Movie* (1978) and *Superman II* (1981)," *Journal of Religion and Film,* vol. 7, no. 1 (April 2003).

Lewis, C.S. *An Experiment in Criticism.* New York: Cambridge University Press, 2002.

———. *God in the Dock*. Grand Rapids, MI: William B. Eerdmans, 1970.

———. *Mere Christianity*. New York: Scribner, 1997.

———. *Miracles*. San Francisco: Harper San Francisco, 2001.

Mankiewicz, Tom. *Superman: The Movie, Expanded Edition* DVD. Burbank, CA: Warner Bros. Home Video, 2000/2001.

Markos, Louis. "Myth Matters," *Christianity Today*, vol. 45, no. 6 (April 23, 2001), p. 32.

Mautner, Michael E. "From the Pit to the Peak: Superman and The Ascension of America," *Thesis* (Nov. 23, 1987). Available online at http://superman. ws/americanway/thesis.php.

Short, Robert. *The Gospel According to Peanuts*. Louisville, KY: Westminster John Knox Press.

———. *The Gospel from Outer Space*. New York: Harper and Row, 1983.

———. *The Parables of Peanuts*. New York: Harper Collins, 2002.

Smith, Sean. "Steely Man," *Newsweek*, vol. 146, issue 11 (September 12, 2005).

Sproul, R.C., Jr. "Myth Became Fact," *New Christendom Journal* (online), issue 10.

Notes

*   *   ✳   *   *

Chapter 2—A Reflection to Be Recognized

1. See, respectively, Genesis 1:1; 2:4; 48:15; Deuteronomy 32:6; 32:15.
2. See Genesis 1:26.
3. See Exodus 31:2-6.
4. Acts 17:28.
5. 1 Corinthians 15:33.
6. Titus 1:12.
7. See, respectively, Psalm 22; Jonah 1:17; Matthew 27:46; John 19:24; Matthew 12:40-41.
8. See Matthew 25:31-46.
9. See Matthew 13:10.
10. See 2 Corinthians 5:18.
11. See Matthew 25:14-28.
12. Matthew 25:24-27.
13. Colossians 1:16-17.
14. Matthew 13:14-15.
15. Matthew 13:16-17.
16. Colossians 1:15.
17. Ecclesiastes 3:11.

Chapter 3—. . . And God Created Superman

1. See Proverbs 8–9.

Chapter 4—The One and Only Son

1. See Genesis 7:11-23.
2. Luke 24:4.
3. Here Muir is referencing imagery from Revelation 12:7-9.
4. See Revelation 16:16-21 for the biblical description of Armageddon.
5. See, respectively, Matthew 13:33 and 13:44.
6. See, respectively, Genesis 35:11; Matthew 1:23.
7. See, respectively, Luke 11:33; Mark 4:22; Matthew 11:25.
8. John 16:13.
9. Genesis 35:15.
10. Philippians 3:20-21.

Chapter 5—The Star Child

1. Matthew 2:2; 2:9.
2. See Luke 10:38-41 KJV.
3. *Sarah*—Genesis 11:30; 18:10-15; 21:1-2; *Rebekah*—Genesis 25:21; *Elizabeth*—Luke 1:7,24; *Manoah's unnamed wife, the mother of Samson*—Judges 13:2-5.
4. See Matthew 1:18-25.
5. 2 Thessalonians 1:7-9.
6. Psalm 31:5.

Chapter 6—"You Are Here for a Reason"

1. Luke 22:41-42; see 22:43.
2. See Luke 23:39.
3. See Luke 23:34.
4. See Luke 23:46,55; 24:6.
5. See Matthew 3:16-17.
6. See Matthew 4:1.
7. See Mark 1:12-13.
8. See, respectively, Luke 4:1; 4:2; Matthew 4:11.
9. See, respectively, Luke 10:18; Matthew 4:6.
10. See Luke 3:23.
11. John 3:16; 8:12.

Chapter 7—A Never-Ending Battle for Truth

1. See Matthew 4:23; 9:25.
2. See Matthew 8:26.
3. See Matthew 14:25.
4. Matthew 11:29.
5. Matthew 16:15.
6. John 14:6 KJV.
7. See Colossians 1:16-17.
8. 1 Corinthians 1:20-24.
9. Romans 1:19-20.
10. John 5:13.
11. Mark 4:33-34.
12. In regard to Jesus' concealing his identity, see, respectively, Mark 1:43-45; 3:12; 5:43.

13. See Matthew 13:53-58.
14. See John 7:3-10.
15. 1 Corinthians 9:20-22.
16. 1 Corinthians 15:42-43.
17. 1 Corinthians 15:49.
18. 1 Corinthians 15:53-54.

Chapter 8—Power in the Blood

1. Matthew 26:53-54.
2. Matthew 5:3
3. Matthew 5:4.
4. Matthew 5:5.
5. Matthew 5:6.
6. See Matthew 5:17.
7. Matthew 5:7.
8. Matthew 5:8.
9. Matthew 5:9
10. Matthew 5:10.
11. For these points, see, respectively, Matthew 3:17; Hebrews 4:14-16; Hebrews 4:13; Revelation 1:14; Matthew 6:7-8; John 4:50-53; Acts 1:9-11.
12. See Romans 3:25-26.
13. See Acts 4:30-31.
14. Acts 9:3-6.

Chapter 9—True Blue

1. Respectively, Numbers 15:38-39; John 6:38.
2. See Matthew 2:11.
3. Respectively, Haggai 2:8-9; Revelation 14:14.
4. Revelation 1:5.
5. 1 Corinthians 13:13.
6. For these six points regarding angels in the Bible, see, respectively, Zechariah 1:8-11; Matthew 18:10; Exodus 14:19, Daniel 6:22, and Acts 12:7-11; Hebrews 1:14; 2 Samuel 24:16; 2 Kings 6:16-18, Daniel 10:12-13, and Revelation 20:1-2.
7. Numbers 21:4-9.
8. 2 Kings 18:4.
9. John 3:14-15.

Chapter 10—A Super Man

1. Matthew 11:19.
2. See Matthew 17:2.
3. Matthew 7:14.
4. See Luke 8:2.
5. Matthew 14:29.
6. Matthew 14:30; 14:31.
7. See John 1:32.
8. John 20:25.
9. See John 11:35.

10. The quotation is referring to, respectively, Matthew 9:23-35; Luke 7:11-15; John 11:41-44.

Chapter 11—Death

1. Isaiah 14:13-15.
2. Matthew 4:8-10.
3. Romans 6:4.
4. See Matthew 28:1-2.
5. In regard to these five points, see, respectively, Matthew 27:51; 1 Peter 3:18-20; Matthew 27:52; Colossians 2:15; Luke 24:51.
6. See John 1:5.
7. See Matthew 10:2-4.
8. Revelation 12:7-9.
9. Revelation 12:4-5.
10. Revelation 20:1-3.
11. See Matthew 26:39-42.
12. Revelation 12:17.
13. Revelation 13:7-8.
14. Psalm 23:2.
15. Revelation 13:2.
16. Revelation 13:4.
17. Revelation 13:11.
18. See Matthew 26:48-49.
19. Revelation 20:10.

Chapter 12—Burial

1. See Exodus 34:29.
2. Revelation 17:8.
3. Hebrews 2:14.
4. 1 Peter 5:8.
5. See John 19:34.
6. Revelation 16:16-19.
7. Luke 23:44.
8. Matthew 28:12-13.
9. See Matthew 1:1.
10. 1 Peter 3;19.
11. Revelation 14:1.

Chapter 13—Resurrection

1. Revelation 6:2.
2. See Genesis 14:4.
3. Revelation 6:4.
4. Revelation 6:5-6.
5. Revelation 6:8.
6. Revelation 13:1.
7. Revelation 13:3.
8. Revelation 13:5-6.
9. Revelation 13:7.

10. Revelation 13:12.
11. Revelation 13:13.
12. Revelation 13:14-15.
13. See Exodus 32:2-4.
14. Matthew 24:4-8.
15. Matthew 24:24.
16. Luke 1:26-31.
17. See John 19:34.
18. Quoted are, respectively, Matthew 27:59; Luke 24:3; 24:12.

Chapter 14—Second Coming

1. Mark 13:25-26.
2. Matthew 24:12-13.
3. Revelation 16:20.
4. Revelation 21:1.

Afterword—Jesus Christ, Superhero

1. Matthew 11:28; 28:20.
2. Revelation 13:8.

HARVEST HOUSE PUBLISHERS

Helping You See God's Truth Wherever It Is

Fearless Faith

Living Beyond the Walls of Safe Christianity

JOHN FISCHER

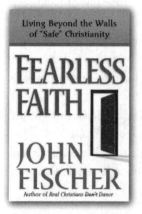

It's not always easy to be a Christian these days. We live in a culture that frequently challenges the very foundations of our faith. Our natural response is to flee from the criticisms and the negative influences that surround us, creating our own safe Christian environment in an unsafe world. But as John Fischer reminds us, that's not what Jesus intended.

We are not called to form a Christian subculture to protect ourselves from being offended or challenged, but to fearlessly engage our culture at every level with the hope and promise of the gospel. In this provocative book, Fischer reminds us that we are to be *in the world*—part of the dialogue—and making a contribution to every area of our lives from a perspective of faith.

Fearless Faith will help those who desire to impact their world...

- understand the true meaning of being "in the world, but not of the world"
- find the courage to bring God's light to life's darkest corners
- learn to recognize the many ways that God is already at work in the world
- change their world by becoming constructively involved in it

*   *   ✱   *   *

"Fast-paced and thought-provoking."

—**Sigmund Brouwer**, bestselling author and coauthor of
The Last Disciple, The Weeping Chamber, and the Mars Diaries

Forgiving Solomon Long

Chris Well

Kansas City—home of the *Star*, the Chiefs, and the blues. Visit. Have the time of your life. Just don't lose it if you meet one of these players at the wrong end of his piece...

Crime boss Frank "Fat Cat" Catalano has dreams of building a legacy in Kansas City—but a coalition of local storeowners and clergy have banded together to try to break his stranglehold.

Detective Tom Griggs is determined to bring Fat Cat down, no matter what the cost. Even if that cost is neglecting—and losing—his own wife.

Hit man Solomon "Solo" Long is a "cleaner" flown in from the coast to make sure the locals get the message from Fat Cat.

It all adds up to a sizzling page-turner that crackles with wit and unexpected heart—and hits you in the gut with a powerful message of forgiveness.

Deliver Us from Evelyn

Chris Well

Kansas City, the heart of America—where the heartless Evelyn Blake lords it over the Blake media empire. The inconvenience she suffers when her billionaire husband, Warren, mysteriously disappears is multiplied when nearly everybody starts inquiring, "Where is Blake?"...

Detectives Tom Griggs and Charlie Pasch are feeling the heat from on high to get this thing solved.

Revenge-focused mobster Viktor Zhukov has figured out Blake was tied in with a rival gang's ambush.

Rev. Damascus Rhodes (his current alias) figures a man of the cloth can properly console the grieving Mrs. Blake.

By the end of this high-speed thriller, some characters find unexpected redemption...and more than a few are begging, *Deliver Us from Evelyn...*

"Clever, snappy, and streetwise!"

—**Creston Mapes**, author of *Dark Star* and *Full Tilt*